Happy
Cooking!

Xo
Gail Hacker

> **IMPORTANT**
>
> The nutritional information in this book is approximate and based on each recipe before additional options are incorporated.

Cover photo: Suzanne Teresa
Back cover photo: Liana Louzon
Lifestyle photos: Amy Wagner
Food photography: Lori Harder
Cover design: Jacqueline Hornyak
Editing, design and layout: Heidi Zeto

contents

about the author

Lori is a fitness expert, fitness model, transformational speaker, author, and wellness and nutrition coach. She owns and operates multiple businesses while balancing a healthy lifestyle, travel and a happy family life. Setting records in her field, Lori became a three-time Fitness World Champion while building her businesses and owning a gym.

Lori strives to be a healthy, motivational role model to others and at all times, feel fit and full of energy. She wants everyone to experience the same amount of happiness and success that comes from feeding your body the healthy (good-tasting) foods it needs to function at the top of its game.

"I refuse to sacrifice taste and my social life," Lori says. "I really believe you can have it all with a little creativity, proper education, preparation and nutrition! If you put great things in your body, your body will perform the way it was intended to, and you will feel and look amazing! Our body is a miracle and when you take care of it, it will take care of you."

Lori lives in California with her husband, Chris and her dog, Waffles. They enjoy being active year-round and sharing the gift of health as their full-time jobs.

special thanks

There are so many people who make my life more blessed than I deserve, so I would like to take a moment to name a few who have made this book possible...

To my mother-in-law, Marie, this would still just be a dream without your brilliance in the kitchen. Thank you for all of your support and hard work on so many recipes and in everything we do. And thank you for seeing the vision and pouring your heart into all of our recipes.

Thanks to my amazing husband and best friend for all of your support in everything I do. The fact that you believe in me makes me feel like I can do anything. Thanks for being my sounding board, taste-tester and partner in dreaming!

Thanks to my mom and dad for teaching me to cook and get creative! I will never forget the memories of hanging out in the kitchen and cooking together. Dad, thanks for eating my entire batch of "cinnamon and sugar cookies" that were actually "cumin and sugar cookies," just so I wouldn't feel bad. And to my mom, I'm sorry that I lied to you about eating all four blueberry muffins. "No mom, I just saw them! They have to be in here somewhere!" It was only because you were such a good cook, and I couldn't resist!

Thanks to my incredible designer/editor, Heidi Zeto, for always being ready for anything I throw at her and making it look fantastic.

Thanks to my friend and registered dietitian, Stacie Hassing, for helping with the meal guides and nutrition analysis, and for always pouring her heart into our projects!

Looking back, it's obvious that my creativity in the kitchen comes from both my mom and dad. Many of my childhood memories revolve around my family cooking together and bonding over great food. My dad even built a separate mini counter for my sister and I so we could cook, too. My parents also made me try at least a bite of everything. They would say, "How on Earth will you know if you don't like it if you never try it?" And so with those words echoing in my brain, down the hatch everything went! I learned not to fear anything when it came to food!

Unfortunately, this "fearlessness" led me down a path of overindulgence. Even as a young kid, I noticed that I felt tired and lethargic from continually eating junk. And what's worse, my clothes started to fit tighter. I knew I had to do something about it. But how was I — a self-proclaimed lover of all foods — going to get in shape and feel better when I had no clue how to begin? And so, my lifelong search for knowledge about health and nutrition began. I was determined to find a way to make healthy meals taste incredible for everyone — especially myself.

Fast forward a whole lot of years, and a lot of trial and error in the healthy cooking department, and the LoriHarder.com idea was born. I will never forget the day the light-bulb moment happened. I was sitting around the table with my husband and mother-in-law eating a delicious, healthy meal. I was rambling on about how I wanted to share my knowledge (and love) with others about staying fit and keeping balance in life despite being crazy busy. Finally, after a lot of back and forth on how I could accomplish this, my mother-in-law, Marie, and I realized we had a great thing to share. With the combination of her hearty home-style cooking background and my healthy, creative background, we have made it our mission to come up with the most delicious, quick and healthy recipes to prove we can fool anyone into eating healthy! [Insert evil laugh here...]

This cookbook, as well as LoriHarder.com, was created out of a desire to be healthy, feel great, look great and have energy — without compromising the taste of food (or the size of your waistline). I know first-hand that if I don't eat healthy food, I won't have the energy to live the life I want. Eating healthy food is truly the secret to staying motivated and energized. And, I want everyone to share this feeling!

You'll find that the recipes are versatile enough that you can eat them at home, take them on the go or make for parties or guests. These foods will keep you feeling energized, full and happy while keeping taste buds content!

Ready to find out for yourself? Set your timers, take control of your health and get ready to enjoy some family favorites sure to please even the toughest food critic! I hope you love these recipes as much as I loved creating them.

Bon appétit!

a note from the author

Hi there!

I just wanted to take the time to say hello and express my deepest gratitude to you for picking up my cookbook. This is not just another "eat my healthy, cardboard recipes" cookbook, this is your get fit, mouth-watering, "fall back in love with your food" guide!

I knew I had to release a revised edition because of all the stories I've heard about people and their families losing weight, feeling better, enjoying food, cooking together and getting their lives back — just by implementing these recipes every day. So this round, I wanted to make sure that you're receiving both new recipes (plus some special holiday recipes to have as tradition for years to come), and a new tool to help create transformation in your life. Whether you want to change your body, energy or mood, this new cookbook edition will rock your world!

As a former overweight child turned fitness cover model, I have dedicated my life to living healthy. But this cookbook represents so much more than healthy recipes. It represents my journey and my passion to feel good, get fit and stay fit — all while balancing life's everyday happenings. I want to share this message of balance and feeling vibrant, present and alive with everyone.

When you feel great, you have the energy to get done all that your busy life entails. Processed foods rob of us of so much more than just our confidence in our bodies. They rob us of our time, energy and happiness. This new way of eating and living will change the way you feel about healthy food. When we eat real food, we start to feel and look the way we were intended to — AMAZING!

These recipes are fast, tasty and easy! And they get their flavor from fruits, veggies, proteins and incredible spices — just the way we were meant to eat! No matter how active you are, your hard work won't show without a consistent healthy diet. We've made it easy by taking the guesswork out of meal planning. Speaking of which, this edition includes a detailed 4-Week Meal Guide to bust you out of that plateau and get you into a body that not only looks great, but FEELS incredible! And who doesn't want that?

I hope this new, revised edition takes you on an amazing journey of discovery as you start your new healthy way of life! I also wanted to give an extra special thanks to those who have supported my passion for the past few years. You have given me an outlet to be creative, and I can't tell you how rewarding it is to see my visions and dreams become a reality. Without all of you this would still be just a wish.

I hope my books will be a part of your life's greatest memories for a long time to come. Please don't hesitate to let me know your thoughts — you are the heart of what I do!

Much Love,

Lori Harder

Lori Harder

lori harder's top 25 spices

One of the most common things I hear from the busy girl trying to cook a healthy and good tasting meal is that they never seem to have the spices or herbs that are called for in a recipe. Herbs and spices are the best way to add a TON of incredible flavor with hardly any calories. So here it is, the 25 spices and herbs every cook should keep in their pantry:

1. **BASIL** (Dried) Common seasoning for meat, fish, tomato dishes, pizza sauce, soups, stews, dressings and salads.

2. **CAYENNE PEPPER** (Ground) Also called red pepper. Most commonly used in Mexican and Italian dishes, Indian foods, chili products, sausage, salsas, dressings and relishes. A very strong spice so must be used in moderation.

3. **CELERY** (Seed or Flakes) Used in stews, soups, fish dishes, salads & dressings, and veggie dishes.

4. **CHILI POWDER** Commonly used in Mexican foods, sauces (such as barbecue & taco sauce) chilis, marinades and dips. This is quite spicy and should be used in moderation.

5. **CHIVES** (Dried or can be chopped & frozen) Have a light onion flavor and are commonly used to flavor dips, sauces, soups, egg dishes, baked potatoes, and veggie dishes. Can be used to replace onion flavor in a recipe. Chives are a good source of potassium, iron and calcium.

6. **CINNAMON** (Ground) Commonly used in spiced beverages, pudding, baked goods, sauces, some soups, meats, chicken, Chinese and Indian dishes.

7. **CILANTRO** (Dried) Commonly used in Mexican dishes, salsas, salad dressings, and sauces. Don't over use in a recipe, people either love the flavor or hate it. Those that hate it say it tastes like dishwater.

8. **CLOVES** (Ground) This is a strong spice to be used in moderation in baked goods, ham, sweet potatoes, baked beans, puddings, soups, sausages and sauces such as barbecue.

9. **CORIANDER** (Ground) Has a sweet musk flavor. Commonly used Mexican dishes, cookies, cakes, biscuits, spiced dishes, cheese dishes, pea soup and pork.

10. **CUMIN** (Ground) Commonly used in Mexican dishes, curry dishes, chilis, soups, stews, and sauces. Has an unique and distinct flavor but really not spicy.

11. **CURRY** (Powder) This is a blend of at least 20 spices and herbs. Commonly used in Indian dishes, poultry, soups, stews, meat dishes and sauces.

12. **DILL** (Weed) Usually used in cottage cheese, soups, chowders, salads, sauerkraut, potato salad, fish, meat sauces, dips and apple pie. Great in egg salad.

13. **FENNEL** (Seed) Commonly used in Italian sausage, pork dishes, fish dishes, squash, sweet pickles, cabbage, pastries, Italian dishes and pizza sauce.

14. **GARLIC** (Powder) Commonly used in hundreds of dishes, especially in Italian cooking, chicken, meat, fish, sauces, breads, dips and salads. Almost as commonly used as salt and pepper. When used in cooking always, add the garlic toward the end because garlic burns very easily and may taste bitter. Also, a must have for the fridge is minced garlic.

15. **GINGER** (Ground) Has a pungent spicy flavor and is used in Oriental and Indian cooking. Also used in dressing, dried fruits, gingerbread and pumpkin pie. A little goes a long way.

16. **ITALIAN SEASONING** (Dried) This seasoning is a combination of marjoram, thyme, rosemary, savory, sage, oregano and basil. It is a perfect base for any Italian dish. Can be used on poultry, beef, fish, and meatloaf. It is great in sauces, dips, dressings, and on veggies. It is considered a good all-around seasoning.

17. **MARJORAM** (Dried) Part of the oregano family but with a sweet nutty flavor. It is usually combined with other herbs and used in potato dishes, soups, stews, poultry seasoning, sauces, Greek dishes, and fish dishes.

18. **NUTMEG** (Ground) A relatively sweet spice that adds that little something special to cheese dishes, soups, stews and creamed foods. Great sprinkle on top of custard, eggnog, and whipped cream. Also used in some sausages and ravioli. It boasts a somewhat strong flavor so should be used in moderation.

19. **ONION POWDER** This is often used in partnership with garlic powder. Can be used in dips, sauces, soups, stews, Italian dishes, Mexican dishes, and casseroles. Use in moderation.

20. **OREGANO** (Dried) Commonly used in Italian specialties such as spaghetti sauces, pizzas, soups, stews, tomatoes, and roasted root veggies. Sprinkle lightly on a grilled cheese sandwich, YUMMY!

21. **PAPRIKA** (Ground, Sweet or Ground, Smoky) Sweet paprika has a mild flavor and is commonly used in cream sauces, salad dressings, egg dishes, and veggie dishes. It is often used as a powder garnish. Smoky paprika has a spicier flavor and adds a hint: of smokiness to Mexican, Italian, and Indian dishes. Adds good flavor to spicy sauces (such as barbecue), ketchup, and sausages.

22. **RED PEPPER FLAKES** (Crushed) Spicy, Spicy, Spicy! Adds bold spicy flavor to pasta sauces, pizza, chilis and sauted veggies. Used in most Italian, Mexican and Asian dishes. Add a few flakes to sweet sauces and cheese dishes for that little something extra. The contrast is great and livens up the sweet and cheese dishes. Be careful when using this spice, it carries a kick!

23. **ROSEMARY** (Crushed) This is a sweet, spicy and fragrant herb with a pungent aroma. Commonly used in meat and poultry dishes, Italian dishes, dressings, soups, and stews.

24. **TARRAGON** (Dried) Has a flavor similar to licorice. Commonly used in sauces, meat, poultry, and fish dishes, salads, herb dressings and tomato casseroles. Has a very pleasant flavor and aroma.

25. **THYME** (Dried) This has a somewhat strong flavor commonly used in stews, tomato based soups and sauces, poultry, meats, sausages and chowders.

Well cooks, this is my spice and herb bible. Don't get overwhelmed. You don't have to go out and buy them all immediately. Just take this list with you to the grocery store and pick up a few at a time. You can find small containers of these spices and herbs at reasonable prices (usually under $1!) in the spice aisle. Before you know it you will have your own spice pantry that can accommodate any recipe. If you find you do not have a specific spice called for in a recipe, chances are you will have a good substitute that will still enhance the recipe.

Have fun experimenting with your spices and herbs. Smell and taste your spices, and then try adding some to your favorite recipes. Just remember not to add too much of any one spice – easy does it in the beginning! Dried and ground herbs and spices are stronger than fresh ones, less expensive and last a lot longer.

Enjoy!

lori harder's lifestyle tips & tricks

1. **Eat more often.** This keeps you from energy crashes, getting tired and making bad food choices. Aim to eat 5 to 6 small meals or 3 average meals and 2 snacks. You may need to work up to eating this often, but keep trying! This is a great way to ensure you'll never get too hungry and make choices that aren't in line with your goals.

2. **Always plan ahead!** Whether you're headed to a party or to the office, the only way to set yourself up in an environment for success is by planning ahead. You must have a plan at all times and bring healthy options whenever possible. Chances are, your friends and family will end up enjoying them, too!

3. **Keep the essentials on hand.** No matter how much planning we do, sometimes life gets in the way. Always keep a few of your favorite Cookbook recipes frozen, individually wrapped, and ready to warm and eat!

4. **This is a lifestyle.** That means you must ease your way into it in order to make sure it's something you can stick with long term. Don't jump head-first and think you'll fall in love with it. Just like anything, change takes getting used to. Start with switching 1 to 2 of your meals each day the first week and add more as time goes on. Soon you'll feel great and start craving clean food all the time!

5. **Move more.** Exercise and muscle help shape your body and eating healthy will reveal it! Don't be afraid to lift some weights to keep your metabolism burning fat and calories. Make your body work for you even when you're not. I love to take a walk after a big meal or if I'm bored and can't seem to stop craving everything under the sun. This helps shift your mood and focus to something unrelated to food. Get your family or walking buddy to join you!

6. **Fill most of your plate with lean protein and veggies.** I don't believe in eliminating carbohydrates or fruit from your diet — EVER! Feeling deprived will always lead to binging. Fill up on veggies, fruits and proteins, and keep the other stuff in moderation.

7. **Make healthier versions of your favorites or keep your portion size small.** If you MUST have some chocolate or pizza, try to make a healthier version. If this doesn't quench the craving, drink a large glass of water and have a small serving of the real thing. Most times, we realize it wasn't as good as we imagined. This also helps keep you from feeling deprived. Remember, this is a lifestyle! If you think you'll never be able to have something again, you'll never feel this lifestyle is maintainable.

8. **Recruit your family and friends.** This is much easier and more fun when the whole family is on board! Ask them what they're in the mood for and see how tasty you can make a healthier version. Involve them and remind them of how great they feel when they eat healthy!

9. **Plan your weekends and vacations around activities.** Oftentimes, we plan our social events around food. This creates a very challenging environment to be healthy in, not to mention it's not a good lesson to teach our children. Try taking a class, a fun new lesson, playing games or heading outside for some family and friend time. There is nothing better than playing outside all day!

10. **Reward yourself with things that don't involve food or drink.** For most everything in our lives, we've rewarded ourselves with a celebration revolving around food and booze. As a result, when we do something good, we associate warm, fuzzy feelings with indulging. In turn, when we try to take the healthier path, we feel like we're missing out. Start celebrating your victories by treating yourself to a concert, ball game, massage, amusement park or a great new outfit!

4 weeks to fabulous
jump start meal guide

TABLE OF CONTENTS

A MESSAGE FROM LORI

Hello!

I am thrilled you have taken the time to put your health first and invest in the most important thing possible — YOU! We all know that without our health we have nothing, and what we put into our bodies is truly what we become. What we feed ourselves reflects in every area of our life — relationships, mood, anxiety, energy, sleep, disease and more. The food we eat can either be what heals us and keeps us healthy, or what ultimately causes our health issues.

Our vision with this delicious, healthy and reasonable meal plan is for you to understand and love the ideas of eating clean, eating often and making smart, maintainable choices. A great meal plan is not great if you can't keep it up for life. My theory has always been — the foods you eat while getting to your goals should be the same foods you eat once you've achieved those goals. This often means that you'll need to make changes to both your lifestyle and eating habits, however, I firmly believe you should never feel deprived or bummed that your food doesn't taste good.

I also believe in finding a balance that works for you. What works for you may not work for others because of body type, height, weight etc. That's where it gets fun — you get to figure out what works best for you. This meal plan may work perfectly for you or you made need to make small tweaks —and that's OK!

As you begin this plan, it's very important to be aware of how you're feeling each day. Keep track of how often you're eating (you should be eating every few hours). If you're super hungry during the day or night after the first week of letting your body adjust, you may need to make portion adjustments. If you're feeling tired or dizzy for any reason, you may need to add in a bit more starch or protein during the day. Whatever it may be, the plan has you covered — just make sure you read EVERYTHING (a few times through) so you know what to do when you're struggling. With that being said, listen to your body!

Make sure you're drinking tons of water and making sleep a priority! Did you know that getting adequate sleep creates your body's own appetite suppressant? How cool is that? The food you eat can't go to work if you don't give your body the fighting chance it needs!

Please remember, this process takes time and their will be a learning curve! Sometimes we're undoing a lifetime of unhealthy eating, bad habits and learning a new pattern. If this is overwhelming, try following just a few meals a day and add small goals each week as you go. Whatever you do, don't give up. This isn't just about what you look like —it's so much more about how you feel, the quality of life you're living and the example you're setting for your loved ones.

This may not be easy at first, and I know you may get comments from friends or family about your new choices. So, I want you to post a list of 10 reasons why you need to do this and 10 reasons why you can no longer live the way you do. Please let your excuses be your new reasons why you must. You need to do this for you, your family, your kids... because you're busy and because you have no time and energy! This will only help improve your life in the most amazing, beautiful and sometimes surprising ways. We are so much more than our bodies, and forgiveness is the first step to healing. No matter what mistakes you've made or how much you feel you've failed, you are only one healthy meal and/or workout away from being back on track! A failure is a much needed lesson on what to look for next time! Use it to your advantage instead of dwelling on it and self sabotaging.

We are here for you, and I am thrilled to introduce my incredible partner, Stacie Hassing, a registered and licensed dietitian who collaborated with me on this incredible project. We share the same vision of getting you to a place of peace with food — a place where it can become nurturing and enjoyable again instead of stressful, confusing or laden with guilt. Food is a blessing, and we want to teach you that you no longer need to be calorie-obsessed and retstrict certain foods. We really want you to find that place where you are comfortable and feel satisfied after a day of food.

We thank you so much and we're so excited to be taking this journey with you!

So much love to all of you! WE WILL DO THIS!

Lori Harder

A MESSAGE FROM STACIE

Hi ladies!

Welcome to the *Lori Harder's 4 Weeks to Fabulous Jump Start Meal Guide!*

Allow me to introduce myself — my name is Stacie Hassing, and I am a registered and licensed dietitian. Teaming up with Lori on this project has been an incredible opportunity, and I am absolutely thrilled to be a part of it. I am so excited to share this meal guide with you! It is my hope that you'll find this to be a helpful tool as you work toward your health and fitness goals, and most importantly, build a healthy relationship with food.

Spreading the word on good health and proper nutrition is a very strong passion of mine. And as such, the below nutrition tips are important to keep in mind as you follow this (or any) guide:

There is no such thing as a "perfect" diet. Everyone's nutritional needs vary, so what works for you may not work for your best friend. It truly comes down to consistency and listening to your body. To create a healthy relationship with food, I encourage you to focus on nourishing your body with REAL and wholesome foods – foods that are nutrient dense and provide you with the energy you need to live life to the fullest. After all, "a healthy outside begins within." Obsessing over counting calories or being overly restrictive can be your worst enemy, and this often leads to developing an unhealthy relationship with food and eventually, may turn into an emotional roller coaster ride. In other words, if you like chocolate, eat chocolate! Just make sure to keep your portion size in check.

I want you to make a promise to yourself that you will never use the word "diet" in terms of "I'm on a diet" or a similar phrase! The word diet, as used in this phrase, screams short-term changes leading to short-term results, which clearly is not what we're looking for. Interestingly enough, the Greek meaning of the word diet is "way of life," so let's put that to action and create a life-long healthy habit!

Lastly, enjoy food! Food is fuel. Try not to put a number on it. In my practice, I have found that individuals who listen to their body, focus on well-balanced eating of REAL and wholesome foods versus traditional calorie counting or points, are the healthiest — mentally and physically. As a result, individuals have more energy, feel more in balance, more confidence, a more positive outlook on life and they are more driven to achieve their physical and life-long goals. To begin, keep a food journal, not to count calories or macros, but to make notes as to how you feel before and after your meal. That's what is most important – how food makes you feel!

I encourage you to use this meal guide to help you find what works best for you. Following this meal guide perfectly is not expected, and I recommend that you alter it to fit your lifestyle and physical needs. We are so excited to lead you down a path of good nutrition because we know nutrition is a key factor in achieving physical results as well as creating a healthy mind and finding balance. Now, fill your kitchen with healthy, wholesome foods, and let's get cooking!

Congrats on committing yourself to a healthier YOU!

With lots of love and good health,

Stacie Hassing, RD, LD

MEAL GUIDE TIPS AND SUGGESTIONS

1. The 4 Weeks to Fabulous Jump Start Meal Guide is intended to be used only as a guideline. Because everyone's needs are different, this meal guide is not an individualized plan and may need to be altered to fit your personal needs and lifestyle. You may choose to add a 6th meal or increase portion sizes — especially if you're exercising and working out daily. The KEY is listening to your body!

2. The goal of the meal guide is to help you learn how to incorporate wholesome and healthy foods in a well-balanced matter. This will provide you with adequate fuel (nutrients) for your workouts and everyday living, as well as enhance results and produce greater amounts of energy.

3. Within the meal guide, if you want to move meals around to better fit your schedule and lifestyle you absolutely can. In addition, you can also do the same week back-to-back, or if you like a particular week, you can continue to follow that plan for as long as you'd like. Just be sure to keep the body guessing with new foods. By making simple changes such as swapping out different fruits, veggies, healthy carbs, or different protein source, etc., you'll be able to do just that – and prevent boredom with your food choices.

4. Food journaling is recommended as it's a helpful way to stay accountable to yourself. When food journaling, keep track of what time you ate, what you ate, how much you ate, any emotions associated with eating, and how you felt after each meal. This will help you discover which foods make you feel best!

5. Meals should be spaced out about every 3 to 4 hours. It is VERY important not to skip meals! Consistent meal intake from day to day will promote stable blood sugars and in turn, enhance metabolism.

6. You'll notice that the serving sizes are listed as ranges, and this is because everyone's needs are different. You know your body best!

7. Feel free to add a side salad or extra veggies to any meal. This cookbook includes several delicious homemade dressing recipes found on pages 64-70.

8. Use the Meal Prep Guide that's included with each week's meal guide. Look at the meal plan for the upcoming week, and plan some time to meal prep and make recipes for the next 3-4 days. Choose one day during the week or weekend that you can spend some time prepping food and planning for the week ahead.

9. You will see that leftovers (L/Os) are included in the weekly meal guides, so you'll want to review the recipes, in case you need to double the recipe or only make half. This will also depend on how many you're cooking for.

10. If you've hit a plateau, try eating mostly green veggies, lean protein, and a good fat at your last meal.

11. Always make sure you're drinking at least half your body weight in ounces of water OR a minimum of 80 oz. of water per day. Hydration is KEY for all aspects of promoting a healthy body!

12. Use each week's grocery list as a way to check off the items you need and those you already have on hand. You may need to make a quick stop at the grocery store during the week, but the bulk of your weekly groceries can be purchased at once. In addition, be sure to look at the Food Staples page, check off the items you already have and make notes of those that you need to purchase. You'll find that it also lists which weeks you'll need particular items.

13. The Italian Turkey Sausage on pg. 121 of Lori Harder's Cookbook is a great go-to recipe. This is an easy recipe that you can always keep on hand and store in the freezer. Don't be afraid to double this recipe!

14. You can also make larger batches of any of the freezer-friendly recipes noted in the meal prep guide. Doubling recipes and freezing them shortens the time spent on future meal preps.

Isagenix®

* Isagenix is Lori's supplement of choice, and you'll see it as an option throughout the meal plan. However, if you have a favorite protein shake recipe or product, you can certainly choose that instead. To learn more about Isagenix and why Lori chooses these products, see "Why Supplementation?" on page 20.

* Additional protein shake recipes are included on pages 160-161.

* Interested in learning more about Isagenix? Contact Lori at hello@busygirlhealthylife.com.

FOOD STAPLES

The number in the right-hand column refers to the week in which the food staple is needed.

Spices/Seasonings	
Salt	1, 2, 3, 4
Pepper	1, 2, 3, 4
Garlic Powder	1, 2, 3, 4
Onion Powder	3
Garlic Salt	3
Italian Seasoning	1, 3
Dried Thyme	1, 2, 3, 4
Dried Basil	4
Dried Rosemary	1, 2, 3, 4
Dried Oregano	1, 3, 4
Dried Parsley	3
Dried Dill Weed	1
Fennel Seed	1, 2, 3
Red Pepper Flakes	1, 2, 3, 4
Chili Powder	1, 4
Paprika/Smokey Paprika	1, 3
Cayenne	1, 2, 3
Nutmeg	1, 3, 4
Cinnamon	1, 2, 4
Ground Ginger	1, 3
Sweeteners/Flavorings/Baking	
Stevia	1, 2, 3, 4
Honey	1, 3, 4
Pure Maple Syrup	1, 2, 4
Baking Soda	2
Baking Powder	2, 4
Pure Vanilla Extract	2
Cocoa Powder	4
Whole Wheat Pastry Flour (~3 cups)	2, 4
Oat Flour (2/3 cup)	2
Mini Chocolate Chips	1, 3, 4
Oils/Vinegars	
Olive Oil	1, 2, 3, 4
Coconut Oil (unrefined is best)	1, 2, 3, 4
Sesame Oil	1, 2
Cooking Spray	1, 2, 3
Red Wine Vinegar	1, 3
White Wine Vinegar	4
Balsamic Vinegar	1, 2, 3, 4
Other	
Garlic Clove	1, 3, 4
Chopped Nuts	1, 2, 3
Slivered Almonds	2, 4
Oats (~2 cups)	2, 4
Raw Almonds or Nuts of Choice	1, 2, 3, 4
Nut or Seed Butter Recommended – *All Natural*	2, 4
Bread *for Bread Crumbs – recommend sprouted-grain or gluten free*	1, 2
Low-Sodium Soy Sauce *or could also use Coconut Aminos for soy-free alternative.*	1, 2
Dressing: *See recipes on pages 64-70 of the Cookbook. Could also use olive oil and vinegar or purchase organic bottled dressing.*	1, 2, 3, 4
Meal Replacement Shakes: *Lori recommends Isagenix. If interested, contact Lori at hello@busygirlhealthylife.com.*	1, 2, 3, 4

Week 1: Lori Harder's Jump Start Meal Guide

WEEK 1	Day 1	Day 2	Day 3	Day 4	Day 5	Day 6	Day 7
Meal 1 *Jump Start Protein Shake recipes on pg. 160-161*	• Meal Replacement Shake OR • Jump Start Protein Shake	• Meal Replacement Shake OR • Jump Start Protein Shake	• Meal Replacement Shake OR • Jump Start Protein Shake	• Meal Replacement Shake OR • Jump Start Protein Shake	• Meal Replacement Shake OR • Jump Start Protein Shake	• Meal Replacement Shake OR • Jump Start Protein Shake	• Meal Replacement Shake OR • Jump Start Protein Shake
Meal 2	**Simply Balanced Lunch** • 4-6 Breakfast Biscuits *(see pg. 25)* • Side salad OR raw veggies of choice • 1-2 Tbsp. dressing *(see pg. 64-70)* • 1/2-1 cup fresh berries *Suggestion: Freeze Breakfast Biscuit L/Os*	**Asian Salmon Salad** • 3-5 oz. L/O Salmon served on a bed of greens with chopped veggies of choice • 1/6-1/4 avocado • 1-2 Tbsp. chopped nuts • 1-2 Tbsp. dressing *(recommendation: Oriental Dressing, pg. 67)* • 1 pear	**Italian Chicken Breast Wrap** • 3-5 oz. L/O Chicken, cubed • 1 tortilla or lettuce leaf (low-carb option) • Veggies of choice • 1-2 Tbsp. cheese • 1/6-1/4 avocado • 1/2-1 cup fresh berries	**Simply Balanced Lunch** • 4-6 L/O Breakfast Biscuits • Side salad OR raw veggies of choice • 1-2 Tbsp. dressing • 1/2-1 cup fresh berries	**Greek Turkey Burger Lettuce Wraps** • 3-4 oz. L/O turkey burger served in a lettuce wrap with tomato, onion, cucumber, feta etc. • 1-2 Tbsp. seasoned plain yogurt • 1/6-1/4 avocado • 1 apple	**"Freestyle" Salad** • 3-5 oz. L/O chicken/meat/ turkey burger served on a bed of greens with chopped veggies of choice • 1/6-1/4 avocado • 1-2 Tbsp. chopped nuts and/or 1-2 Tbsp. cheese • 1-2 Tbsp. dressing • 1 pear	L/O Meal Well-balanced! • Protein • Carbs • Healthy Fat
Meal 3 *Jump Start Protein Shake recipes on pg. 160-161*	• Meal Replacement Shake OR • Jump Start Protein Shake OR • Option from Meal Alternative list *(pg. 19)*	• Meal Replacement Shake OR • Jump Start Protein Shake OR • Option from Meal Alternative list *(pg. 19)*	• Meal Replacement Shake OR • Jump Start Protein Shake OR • Option from Meal Alternative list *(pg. 19)*	• Meal Replacement Shake OR • Jump Start Protein Shake OR • Option from Meal Alternative list *(pg. 19)*	• Meal Replacement Shake OR • Jump Start Protein Shake OR • Option from Meal Alternative list *(pg. 19)*	• Meal Replacement Shake OR • Jump Start Protein Shake OR • Option from Meal Alternative list *(pg. 19)*	• Meal Replacement Shake OR • Jump Start Protein Shake OR • Option from Meal Alternative list *(pg. 19)*
Meal 4	**Asian Salmon Salad** • 3-5 oz. Asian Salmon (see pg. 140) • Sautéed Asparagus Spears *(Suggestion: Sauté in a little coconut oil with fresh garlic and onion)* • 1/3-2/3 cup rice (optional starch)	**Italian Chicken Breast Wrap** • 3-5 oz. Italian-Marinated Chicken Breast (see pg. 106) • Italian Green Beans (see pg. 88) • 1/2-1 small sweet potato (optional starch)	**Build Your Own Veggie-Loaded Omelet** • 4-6 egg whites or 2-3 whole eggs • Sautéed veggies of choice OR L/O Green Beans or Asparagus • 1-2 Tbsp. cheese • 1/2-1 small sweet potato (optional starch) *Suggestion: Add Italian Turkey Sausage (see pg. 121)*	**Greek Turkey Burger Lettuce Wraps** • 3-4 oz. Turkey Burger *(see pg. 119)* • Served in a lettuce wrap with tomato, onion, cucumber, feta, etc. • 1-2 Tbsp. cheese • 1/6-1/4 avocado • Butternut Squash Fries (see pg. 93)	**Go-To Balanced Meal** • 3-5 oz. Meat (grilled, baked, stir fried or sautéed) • 3/4-1½ cups roasted veggies *(Suggestion: See Simple Roasted Vegetables recipes on pg. 84)* • side salad • 1-2 Tbsp. dressing	**Build Your Own Veggie Loaded Scramble (Wrap)** • 4-6 egg whites or 2-3 whole eggs • Sautéed Veggies of choice OR L/O Roasted Veggies (be generous!) • 1-2 Tbsp. cheese • L/O Butternut Squash Fries or tortilla (optional starch) *Suggestion: Add Italian Turkey Sausage*	**Meal of your choice** • Plan ahead • Use portion control • Enjoy!
Meal 5 *Optional meal – you choose where it fits best*	**Curing a Sweet Tooth!** • 1/2-3/4 cup plain Greek yogurt • 1/4 cup diced apples • 1-2 Tbsp. chopped nuts + a few chocolate chips • Drizzle of honey and a dash of cinnamon	**Cottage Cheese Cucumber Slices** • 1/2-3/4 cup cottage cheese served on top of sliced cucumbers • 15-20 raw almonds	**Super Simple Snack** • Raw veggies of choice • 2 Tbsp.–1/4 cup hummus • 15-20 raw almonds	**Curing a Sweet Tooth!** • 1/2-3/4 cup plain Greek yogurt • 1/4 cup diced apples • 1-2 Tbsp. chopped nuts + a few chocolate chips • Drizzle of honey and a dash of cinnamon	**Cottage Cheese Cucumber Slices** • 1/2-3/4 cup cottage cheese served on top of sliced cucumbers • 15-20 raw almonds	**Super Simple Snack** • Raw veggies of choice • 2 Tbsp.–1/4 cup hummus • 15-20 raw almonds	**Curing a Sweet Tooth!** • 1/2-3/4 cup plain Greek yogurt • 1/4 cup diced apples • 1-2 Tbsp. chopped nuts + a few chocolate chips • Drizzle of honey and a dash of cinnamon

If you prefer, you can enjoy Meal 5 between Meals 1 and 2. Meal 5 is optional and can be consumed whenever you feel you need a little pick-me-up or extra nourishment.

L/O = Leftover

Isagenix is Lori's recommended meal replacement shake. For questions regarding Isagenix products, contact Lori at hello@busygirlhealthylife.com.

WEEK 1: GROCERY LIST

1st Day Item Is Needed	Groceries	Quantity	Recommendations/Notes
Produce			
Day 1	Sweet Onion	1	For Breakfast Biscuits
Day 1	Raw Veggies of Choice	1	Always keep on hand, washed and pre-chopped for an easy snack or add-in to eggs, salads, for sautéing or roasting.
Day 1	Salad Greens	2 large bags or containers	Add a side salad to any meal! Spinach, arugula, kale, romaine etc.
Day 1	Asparagus	1 lb.	Serve with salmon – use leftovers in eggs.
Day 2	Avocado	2	Healthy Fats! Add to a salad or to eggs.
Day 2	Green Beans	1 lb.	For Italian Green Beans
Day 2	Red Onion	1	For Italian Green Beans
Day 2	Portobello Mushroom	6 oz.	For Italian Green Beans
Day 2	Cucumber	2 bags	Always have on hand for easy veggie option.
Day 3	Lettuce Leaf	1 head	For Lettuce Wraps – To keep, store in airtight container with paper towels to absorb liquid.
Day 4	Tomato	1	For Greek Turkey Burger (optional)
Day 2	Sweet Potato	2 medium	Healthy carb!
Day 4	Butternut Squash	1 medium	For Butternut Squash Fries
Day 1	Berries	2-3 cups	Fresh or frozen
Day 1	Orange	1 large	For Asian Salmon (need 1/3 cup juice)
Day 1	Apple	3 small	For snacks and lunches – organic is best.
Day 2	Pear	2	For lunches – organic is best.
Protein/Dairy			
Day 1	Eggs	2 dozen	Organic/pasture-raised is best — high in Omega 3s & fatty acids. For Breakfast Biscuits and evening meals.
Day 1	Turkey Bacon	6 oz.	For Breakfast Biscuits
Day 1	Salmon	1 lb.	For Asian Salmon – wild-caught is best.
Day 2	Chicken Breast	1 lb.	For Italian Chicken. <90 mg of sodium.
Day 4	Lean Ground Turkey	1 lb.	For Greek Turkey Burgers
Day 5	Meat of Choice	1 lb.	Suggestions: Wild-Caught Salmon, Pork Loin, Chicken, Sirloin or Filet.
Day 1	Buttermilk	1/4 cup	For Breakfast Biscuits
Day 1	Cottage Cheese	1 large container	Suggestion: Kalona Super Natural (lowest in sodium) or Organic Valley if available.
Day 1	Sharp Cheddar Cheese	1 block or bag	For Breakfast Biscuits – can also add to salads/eggs. Lori recommends 2%.
Day 1	Plain Greek Yogurt	3 (6 oz.) containers	Suggestions: Fage, Siggi's, Super Natural Kalona or Dreaming Cow
Day 2	Grated Parmesan Cheese	2 Tbsp.	For Italian Green Beans – can also add to salads/eggs.
Day 4	Feta Cheese	1/4 cup	For Greek Turkey Burgers – can also add to salads and eggs.
Breads/Grains			
Day 3	Sprouted Grain or Gluten-Free Tortillas	1 pack	Suggestion: Food for Life brand – store in freezer. (optional item)
Day 1	Rice	1 cup	Optional starch – white, brown or wild rice
Dry/Canned Goods			
Day 1	Mini Chocolate Chips	1 bag	For adding to yogurt to help cure sweet tooth. Store in freezer.
Day 2	Petite Diced Canned Tomatoes	1 (15 oz.) can	For Italian Green Beans
Day 3	Hummus	1 container	For Super Simple Snack
Day 4	Kalamata Olives	Small can/jar	For Greek Turkey Burger – need 1/4 cup
Day 4	Green Olives	Small can/jar	For Greek Turkey Burger – need 1/4 cup
Day 4	Walnuts, chopped	1/4 cup	For Greek Turkey Burger

*   If cooking for others, you may need to adjust quantities.

** If not using a meal replacement shake for Meals 1 and 3, you will need to add those ingredients to your list for snacks and morning shakes.

WEEK 1: MEAL PREP GUIDE

Prepping foods on the weekend is a great way to save time during the week. Here are some items you could prep for week 1!

Recipe or Items to Prep	Suggestions	✓ When Completed
Breakfast Biscuits (pg. 25)	• Make Breakfast Biscuits and portion out 4-6 per serving. • Set aside what you will need for the week. • Freeze the remaining biscuits for future meal preps.	
Asian Salmon (pg. 140)	• Make marinade. • 20 minutes before baking, add salmon per recipe directions.	
Italian-Marinated Chicken Breast (pg. 106)	• Make marinade. • 1-24 hours before baking, add chicken per recipe directions.	
Greek Turkey Burger (pg. 119)	• Prep and chop all of the ingredients. • On day 4 of meal guide, before grilling, simply combine thawed turkey with ingredients.	
Raw Veggies	• Go through the Week 1 Meal Guide, and wash, prep, and chop all raw veggies so they're ready to be eaten or added to recipes for the week ahead.	
Portion Out Items	• Portion out the following items in bags or individual containers for an easy grab-and-go option. – Almonds (15-20) – Yogurt (1/2-3/4 cup) – Cottage Cheese (1/2-3/4 cup) – Berries (1/2-1 cup) – Side Salads – Hummus (2 Tbsp.-1/4 cup)	
Optional: Italian Turkey Sausage (pg. 121)	• Make turkey sausage and freeze. • This recipe makes for an easy, tasty and quality protein addition to dishes such as eggs or salads. • *Add ground turkey to grocery list if you choose to make the sausage.*	

"One must eat to live, not live to eat." – Moliere

WEEK 2	Day 1	Day 2	Day 3	Day 4	Day 5	Day 6	Day 7
Meal 1 *Jump Start Protein Shake recipes on pg. 160-161*	• Meal Replacement Shake OR • Jump Start Protein Shake	• Meal Replacement Shake OR • Jump Start Protein Shake	• Meal Replacement Shake OR • Jump Start Protein Shake	• Meal Replacement Shake OR • Jump Start Protein Shake	• Meal Replacement Shake OR • Jump Start Protein Shake	• Meal Replacement Shake OR • Jump Start Protein Shake	• Meal Replacement Shake OR • Jump Start Protein Shake

If you prefer, you can enjoy Meal 5 between Meals 1 and 2. Meal 5 is optional and can be consumed whenever you feel you need a little pick-me-up or extra nourishment.

WEEK 2	Day 1	Day 2	Day 3	Day 4	Day 5	Day 6	Day 7
Meal 2	**Santa Fe Wrap (or Salad)** • 1 Santa Fe Wrap *(see pg. 112)* • Serve in a tortilla or on a bed of greens for lower-carb option • 1/6-1/4 avocado • 1 orange	**Chinese Casserole** • 1 serving L/O Chinese Casserole served on a bed of spinach • 1-2 Tbsp. sliced or slivered almonds • 1/2-1 cup fresh berries	**Santa Fe Wrap (or Salad)** • 1 Santa Fe Wrap • Serve in a tortilla or on a bed of greens for lower carb option • 1/6-1/4 avocado • 1 orange	**Maple Pecan Chicken Breast Salad** • 3-5 oz. L/O Chicken, cubed and served on a bed of greens with chopped veggies of choice • 1-2 Tbsp. cheese of choice • 1-2 Tbsp. chopped nuts • 1-2 Tbsp. dressing *(see pg. 64-70)* • 1 orange	**Santa Fe Wrap (or Salad)** • 1 Santa Fe Wrap • Serve in a tortilla or on a bed of greens for lower-carb option • 1/6-1/4 avocado • 1 orange	**Broccoli Mushroom Onion Frittata** • 1/4 of L/O Frittata • Side salad • 1-2 Tbsp. dressing • 1/2-1 cup fresh berries	L/O Meal Well-balanced! • Protein • Carbs • Healthy Fat
Meal 3 *Jump Start Protein Shake recipes on pg. 160-161*	• Meal Replacement Shake OR • Jump Start Protein Shake OR Option from Meal Alternative list *(pg. 19)*	• Meal Replacement Shake OR • Jump Start Protein Shake OR Option from Meal Alternative list *(pg. 19)*	• Meal Replacement Shake OR • Jump Start Protein Shake OR Option from Meal Alternative list *(pg. 19)*	• Meal Replacement Shake OR • Jump Start Protein Shake OR Option from Meal Alternative list *(pg. 19)*	• Meal Replacement Shake OR • Jump Start Protein Shake OR Option from Meal Alternative list *(pg. 19)*	• Meal Replacement Shake OR • Jump Start Protein Shake OR Option from Meal Alternative list *(pg. 19)*	• Meal Replacement Shake OR • Jump Start Protein Shake
Meal 4	**Chinese Casserole** • 1 serving Chinese Casserole *(see pg. 124)* • Serve on a bed of spinach • 1-2 Tbsp. sliced or slivered almonds	**Go-To Balanced Meal** • 3-5 oz. Meat (grilled, baked, stir fried or sautéed) • 3/4-1½ cups roasted veggies *(Suggestion: See Simple Roasted Vegetables on pg. 84)* • side salad • 1-2 Tbsp. dressing	**Maple Pecan Chicken** • 3-5 oz. Maple Pecan Chicken Breast *(see pg. 110)* • Steamed or sautéed broccoli or veggies of choice • 1/2-1 small sweet potato *(optional starch)*	**Broccoli Mushroom Onion Frittata** • 1/4 of Frittata *(see pg. 33)* • Side salad • 1-2 Tbsp. dressing • 1 slice toast or 1/2-1 small L/O sweet potato *(optional starch)*	**Go-To Balanced Meal** • 3-5 oz. Meat (grilled, baked, stir fried or sautéed) • 3/4-1½ cups roasted veggies *(Suggestion: See Simple Roasted Vegetables on pg. 84)* • side salad • 1-2 Tbsp. dressing	**"Freestyle" Salad or Wrap** • 3-5 oz. L/O chicken/meat/turkey burger served on a bed of greens with chopped veggies of choice • 1-2 Tbsp. chopped nuts • 1-2 Tbsp. cheese • 1-2 Tbsp. dressing • Tortilla *(optional starch)*	**Meal of your choice** • Plan ahead • Use portion control • Enjoy!
Meal 5 *Optional meal – you choose where it fits best*	**Banana Nut Pancakes** • 1/2-1 serving Banana Nut Pancake recipe *(see pg. 22)* • 1-1½ Tbsp. nut or seed butter • 1/2-1 cup fresh berries	**On-the-Go Snack** • 3-5 Egg whites or 1-2 whole eggs • Celery with 1-1½ Tbsp. nut or seed butter	**It's Like Dessert!** • 1 Mango Cream Muffin *(see pg. 30)* • 15-20 Almonds	**Banana Nut Pancakes** • 1/2-1 serving Banana Nut Pancake recipe • 1-1½ Tbsp. nut or seed butter • 1/2-1 cup fresh berries	**On-the-Go Snack** • 3-5 egg whites or 1-2 whole eggs • Celery with 1-1½ Tbsp. nut or seed butter	**It's Like Dessert!** • 1 Mango Cream Muffin • 15-20 Almonds	**Banana Nut Pancakes** • 1/2-1 serving Banana Nut Pancake recipe • 1-1½ Tbsp. nut or seed butter • 1/2-1 cup fresh berries

L/O = Leftover

*Isagenix is Lori's recommended meal replacement shake. For questions regarding Isagenix products, contact Lori at hello@busygirlhealthylife.com.

WEEK 2: GROCERY LIST

1st Day Item Is Needed	Groceries	Quantity	Recommendations/Notes
Produce			
Day 1	Red Bell Pepper	1	For Santa Fe Wraps
Day 1	Sweet Onion	2	For recipes
Day 1	Corn	1 cup	For Santa Fe Wraps. Can use frozen.
Day 1	Avocado	1	Healthy fats! Add to Santa Fe Wrap.
Day 1	Salad Greens	1 large bag or container	Add a side salad to any meal! Spring mix, arugula, kale, romaine etc.
Day 1	Spinach	1 bag	For serving on top of Chinese Caserole
Day 1	Celery	1 small bunch	For Chinese Casserole and Meal 5
Day 1	Cabbage	2 cups shredded	For Chinese Casserole
Day 2	Raw Veggies of Choice	Variety	Always keep on hand, washed and pre-chopped for an easy snack and easy add-ins to eggs, salads, for sautéing or roasting.
Day 3	Broccoli	1 large head	For serving with Maple Pecan Chicken and for Broccoli Mushroom Onion Frittata
Day 3	Sweet Potato	2 medium	Healthy carb! For optional starch side dish.
Day 1	Fresh Berries	2 (6 oz.) containers	Fresh or frozen. If frozen, make sure there isn't any added sugars.
Day 1	Orange	3	For lunches. Can also be fruit of choice.
Day 1	Banana	1 medium	For pancakes
Day 1	Lime	1	For Santa Fe Wraps
Day 3	Mangos	2 cups	Frozen and diced. For Mango Cream Muffins
Protein/Dairy			
Day 1	Eggs	2 dozen	Organic/pasture-raised is best — high in Omega 3s & fatty acids. For Broccoli Mushroom Onion Frittata.
Day 1	Chicken Breast	2 lbs.	For Santa Fe Wraps and Maple Pecan Chicken. <90 mg of sodium
Day 1	Lean Ground Turkey	1 lb.	For Chinese Casserole
Day 2	Meat of Choice	2 lbs.	Suggestions: Wild-Caught Salmon, Pork Loin, Chicken, Sirloin or Filet.
Day 1	Plain Greek Yogurt	14 oz.	Suggestions: Fage, Siggi's, Super Natural Kalona or Dreaming Cow. For Santa Fe Wraps and Mango Cream Muffins (can also use sour cream for muffins).
Day 1	Cottage Cheese	3/4 cup	Suggestion: Kalona Super Natural (lowest in sodium) or Organic Valley if available.
Day 3	Buttermilk	1/4 cup	For Mango Cream Muffins
Day 4	Cheese of Choice	1 bag/block	May have cheese left over from Week 1.
Day 3	Butter	3 Tbsp.	For Mango Cream Muffins
Day 4	Laughing Cow Swiss Cheese	3 wedges	For Broccoli Mushroom Onion Frittata. Could also use 1/4 cup leftover cheese from Week 1.
Breads/Grains			
Day 1	Tortillas	1 pack	For Santé Fe Wraps. Recommend sprouted grain, whole wheat or gluten free.
Day 1	Rice	3/4 cup	For Chinese Casserole
Dry/Canned Goods			
Day 1	Canned Black Beans	1 (15 oz.) can	For Santa Fe Wraps. Low sodium.
Day 1	Canned Diced Tomatoes with Green Chilies	1 (10 oz.) can	For Santa Fe Wraps.
Day 1	Salsa Verde	1 jar	For Santa Fe Wraps.
Day 1	Beef Broth	2 cups	For Chinese Casserole. Low sodium.
Day 1	Water Chestnuts	1 (8 oz.) can	For Chinese Casserole.
Day 1	Hoisin Sauce	1 Tbsp.	For Chinese Casserole
Day 1	Oats	1 cup	For Banana Pancakes
Day 1	Nut and Seed Butter	1 jar	All natural. Check ingredients.
Day 1	Sliced and Slivered Almonds	1/2 cup	For Chinese Casserole
Day 3	Chopped Pecans	1/4 cup	For Maple Pecan Chicken
Day 4	Canned Mushrooms	1 (4 oz.) can	For Broccoli Mushroom Onion Frittata
Day 3	Whole-Wheat Pastry Flour	1¼ cup	For Mango Cream Muffins. Can purchase in bulk at co-op.
Day 3	Oat Flour	2/3 cup	For Mango Cream Muffins. Can purchase in bulk or grind your own oatmeal.

* If cooking for others, you may need to adjust quantities.

** If not using a meal replacement shake for Meals 1 and 3, you will need to add those ingredients to your list for snacks and morning shakes.

WEEK 2: MEAL PREP GUIDE

Prepping foods on the weekend is a great way to save time during the week. Here are some items you could prep for week 2!

Recipe or Items to Prep	Suggestions	✓ When Completed
Santa Fe Wraps (pg. 112)	• Make chicken filling for Santa Fe Wraps. • Fill wraps with chicken before eating. • Can serve Santa Fe Chicken mixture on a bed of greens.	
Banana Nut Pancakes (pg. 22)	• Make 2 servings of banana pancakes. • Could also make more and freeze for future meal preps or for a quick grab-and-go snack.	
Mango Cream Muffins (pg. 30)	• Make muffins and store in refrigerator. • Could also freeze half of batch for future meal preps.	
Chinese Casserole (pg. 124)	• To make this a quick meal option, either prepare the entire meal and re-heat **OR** prep and chop all of the ingredients, and cook the rice so you can get this dish on the table in no time.	
Maple Pecan Chicken (pg. 110)	• Make pecan breading for chicken.	
Hard-Boiled Eggs	• Hard-boil 6-12 eggs for the week ahead.	
Raw Veggies	• Go through the Week 2 meal guide, and wash, prep, and chop all raw veggies so they're ready to be eaten or added to recipes for the week ahead.	

Portion Out Items	• Portion out the following items in bags or individual containers for an easy grab-and-go option.
	  – Almonds (15-20)
	  – Yogurt (1/2-3/4 cup)
	  – Berries (1/2-1 cup)
	  – Side Salads
	  – Pancakes
	  – Muffins	

Optional: Italian Turkey Sausage (pg. 121)	• Make turkey sausage and freeze. • This recipe makes for an easy, tasty and quality protein addition to dishes such as eggs or salads. • *Add ground turkey to grocery list if you choose to make the sausage.*	

Week 3: Lori Harder's Jump Start Meal Guide

WEEK 3	Day 1	Day 2	Day 3	Day 4	Day 5	Day 6	Day 7
Meal 1 *Jump Start Protein Shake recipes on pg. 160-161*	• Meal Replacement Shake OR • Jump Start Protein Shake	• Meal Replacement Shake OR • Jump Start Protein Shake	• Meal Replacement Shake OR • Jump Start Protein Shake	• Meal Replacement Shake OR • Jump Start Protein Shake	• Meal Replacement Shake OR • Jump Start Protein Shake	• Meal Replacement Shake OR • Jump Start Protein Shake	• Meal Replacement Shake OR • Jump Start Protein Shake

If you prefer, you can enjoy Meal 5 between Meals 1 and 2. Meal 5 is optional and can be consumed whenever you feel you need a little pick-me-up or extra nourishment.

WEEK 3	Day 1	Day 2	Day 3	Day 4	Day 5	Day 6	Day 7
Meal 2	**Salad Niçoise** • 1 serving of Salad Niçoise (see pg. 56) • 1/6-1/4 avocado OR • 1-2 Tbsp. chopped nuts • 1/2-1 cup fresh berries	**Italian Burgers** • 1 Italian Burger (see pg. 120) • Serve with pizza sauce and a little cheese on a bun (skip bun for lower-carb option or only use half of bun) • large side salad • 1-2 Tbsp. dressing • 1 apple	**Salad Niçoise** • 1/4 serving of L/O Salad Niçoise • 1/6-1/4 avocado or • 1-2 Tbsp. chopped nuts • 1/2-1 cup fresh berries	**Green Curry Lettuce Cups** • 2-3 L/O Green Curry Lettuce Cups • 1-2 Tbsp. slivered or sliced almonds • 1 apple	**"Freestyle" Salad or Wrap** • 3-5 oz. L/O chicken/meat/turkey burger served on a bed of greens with chopped veggies of choice • 1/6-1/4 avocado • 1-2 Tbsp. chopped nuts • 1/2-1 cup fresh berries	**Chicken Pizzaioli** • 1 serving of L/O Chicken Pizzaioli • side salad • 1-2 Tbsp. dressing • 1 apple	**L/O Meal** Well-balanced! • Protein • Carbs • Healthy Fat
Meal 3 *Jump Start Protein Shake recipes on pg. 160-161*	• Meal Replacement Shake OR • Jump Start Protein Shake OR Option from Meal Alternative list (pg. 19)	• Meal Replacement Shake OR • Jump Start Protein Shake OR Option from Meal Alternative list (pg. 19)	• Meal Replacement Shake OR • Jump Start Protein Shake OR Option from Meal Alternative list (pg. 19)	• Meal Replacement Shake OR • Jump Start Protein Shake OR Option from Meal Alternative list (pg. 19)	• Meal Replacement Shake OR • Jump Start Protein Shake OR Option from Meal Alternative list (pg. 19)	• Meal Replacement Shake OR • Jump Start Protein Shake OR Option from Meal Alternative list (pg. 19)	• Meal Replacement Shake OR • Jump Start Protein Shake OR Option from Meal Alternative list (pg. 19)
Meal 4	**Italian Burgers** • 1 Italian Burger (see pg. 120) • Serve with pizza sauce and a little cheese on a bun (skip bun for lower-carb option or only use half of bun) • large side salad • 1-2 Tbsp. dressing	**Build Your Own Veggie-Loaded Omelet** • 4-6 egg whites or • 2-3 whole eggs • Sautéed veggies of choice OR L/O Green Beans or Asparagus • 1-2 Tbsp. cheese • 1/2-1 small sweet potato (optional starch) Suggestion: Add Italian Turkey Sausage (see pg. 121)	**Green Curry Lettuce Cups** • 2-3 Green Curry Lettuce Cups (see pg. 98) • 1-2 Tbsp. slivered or sliced almonds • 1/3-2/3 cup rice or quinoa (optional starch)	**Go-To Balanced Meal** • 3-5 oz. Meat (Grill, Baked, Stir Fried or Sautéed) • 3/4-1½ cups roasted veggies (Suggestion: See Simple Roasted Vegetables on pg. 84) • side salad • 1-2 Tbsp. dressing	**Chicken Pizzaioli** • 1 serving of Chicken Pizzaioli (see pg. 109) • side salad • 1-2 Tbsp. dressing • 1 apple	**Build Your Own Veggie-Loaded Omelet** • 4-6 egg whites or • 2-3 whole eggs • Sautéed veggies of choice OR L/O Green Beans or Asparagus • 1-2 Tbsp. cheese • 1/2-1 small sweet potato (optional starch) Suggestion: Add Italian Turkey Sausage	**Meal of your choice** • Plan ahead • Use portion control • Enjoy!
Meal 5 *Optional meal – you choose where it fits best*	**Yummy Hard-Boiled Eggs** • 2-3 Bacon, Tomato & Chive Deviled Eggs (see pg. 43) • 1 apple	**Curing a Sweet Tooth!** • 1/2-3/4 cup plain Greek yogurt • 1/4 cup berries • 1-2 Tbsp. chopped nuts + a few chocolate chips • Drizzle of honey and dash of nutmeg	**Yummy Hard-Boiled Eggs** • 2-3 Bacon, Tomato, and Chive Deviled Eggs • 1 apple	**Cheese Please!** • 1 oz. cheese of choice or 1/2-3/4 cup cottage cheese • raw veggies • 2 Tbsp.–1/4 cup hummus	**Yummy Hard-Boiled Eggs** • 2-3 Bacon, Tomato, and Chive Deviled Eggs • 1 apple	**Curing a Sweet Tooth!** • 1/2-3/4 cup plain Greek yogurt • 1/4 cup berries • 1-2 Tbsp. chopped nuts + a few chocolate chips • Drizzle of honey and dash of nutmeg	**Cheese Please!** • 1 oz. cheese of choice or 1/2-3/4 cup cottage cheese • raw veggies • 2 Tbsp.–1/4 cup hummus

L/O = Leftover

*Isagenix is Lori's recommended meal replacement shake. For questions regarding Isagenix products, contact Lori at hello@busygirlhealthylife.com.

WEEK 3: GROCERY LIST

1st Day Item Is Needed	Groceries	Quantity	Recommendations/Notes
Produce			
Day 1	Green Beans	1 cup	For Salad Nicoise
Day 1	Red Potatoes	2	For Salad Nicoise
Day 1	Red Onion	2 small	For Salad Nicoise and Chicken Pizzaioli
Day 1	Red Bell Pepper	1	For Salad Nicoise
Day 1	Tomatoes	2 medium	For Salad Nicoise and Deviled Eggs
Day 1	Romaine Salad Greens	4 cups 1 container	For Salad Nicoise. For additional side salads. Spring mix, arugula, kale, spinach, etc.
Day 1	Avocado	2	Healthy fats! Add to Santa Fe Wrap.
Day 1	Fresh Chives	1 Tbsp.	For Deviled Eggs – If you are unable to find fresh chives you may substitute with dried chives: 1 tsp. dried chives = 1 Tbsp. fresh chives
Day 2	Raw Veggies of Choice	Variety	Always keep on hand, washed and pre-chopped for an easy snack and easy add-ins to eggs, salads, for sautéing or roasting.
Day 2	Asparagus	1 lb.	For veggies side dish
Day 1	Fresh Mushrooms	1/2 cup	For Italian Turkey Burgers
Day 3	Green Onions	3	For Green Curry Lettuce Wraps
Day 3	Shredded Cabbage	1 cup	For Green Curry Lettuce Wraps
Day 3	Bibb Lettuce or Lettuce Leaf	1 bunch	For Green Curry Lettuce Wraps – can use leftover lettuce for salads.
Day 5	Fresh Basil	2 Tbsp.	For Chicken Pizzaioli – If you are unable to find fresh basil you may with dried basil. 2 tsp. of dried basil = 2 Tbsp. fresh basil.
Day 2	Sweet Potato	2 medium	Healthy carb! For optional starch side dish.
Day 1	Lemon	1	For Greek Dressing
Day 1	Berries	2 containers	Fresh or frozen
Day 1	Apples	7 small	For snacks and lunches
Day 3	Lime	1	For Greek Curry Lettuce Wraps
Protein/Dairy			
Day 1	Eggs	2 dozen	Organic/pasture-raised is best — high in Omega 3s & fatty acids. For Deviled Eggs, omelets/scrambles, Salad Nicoise
Day 1	Canned Tuna	2 (6 oz.) cans	For Salad Nicoise
Day 1	Lean Ground Turkey	1 lb.	For Italian Turkey Burgers – can also use ground beef or chicken.
Day 1	Turkey Bacon	4-5 strips	For Deviled Eggs
Day 3	Chicken Breast	2 lbs.	For Green Curry Chicken Wraps and Chicken Pizzaioli. <90 mg. of sodium
Day 4	Meat of Choice	2 lbs.	Suggestions: Wild-caught fish, pork loin, chicken, sirloin or filet.
Day 1	Mozzarella Cheese	1 block	For Italian Turkey Burgers and Chicken Pizzaioli.
Day 1	Plain Greek Yogurt	1 large container	Suggested Brands: Fage, Siggi's, Super Natural Kalona or Dreaming Cow. For Deviled Eggs and Snacks.
Day 2	Cheese of Choice	1 bag/block	May have cheese left over from Week 1.
Day 4	Cottage Cheese *(optional)*	1 small container	Suggested Brand: Kalona Super Natural or Organic Valley if available. Optional for snack (meal 5)
Breads/Grains			
Day 1	Sprouted-Grain Bread/Buns or Gluten Free	1 pack	Optional for burgers and other meals in week 3.
Day 3	Rice or Quinoa	1 cup	Optional side starch with Green Curry Lettuce Wraps
Dry/Canned Goods			
Day 1	Black/Kalamata Olives	1/2 cup	For Salad Nicoise
Day 1	Chicken Stock/Broth	1/4 cup	For Greek Salad Dressing – freeze leftover stock and use to make dressing in the future.
Day 1	Pizza Sauce	1 small can	For Turkey Burgers
Day 1	Mayonnaise	1 small jar	For Deviled Eggs – can use additional Greek yogurt.
Day 1	Dijon Mustard	1 small jar	For Deviled Eggs
Day 3	Organic Canned Coconut Milk	1/3 cup	For Green Curry Lettuce Wraps
Day 3	Water Chestnuts	1 (8 oz.) can	For Green Curry Lettuce Wraps
Day 3	Green Curry Paste	1 Tbsp.	For Green Curry Lettuce Wraps
Day 4	Hummus	1 container	For Meal 5
Day 5	Crushed Tomatoes	1 (28 oz.) can	For Chicken Pizzaioli
Day 3	Sliced or Slivered Almonds	1/2 cup	For Green Curry Lettuce Wraps
Day 1	Mini Chocolate Chips	1/2 cup	For Yogurt Parfaits – Use L/Os from Week 1

* If cooking for others, you may need to adjust quantities.

** If not using a meal replacement shake for Meals 1 and 3, you will need to add those ingredients to your list for snacks and morning shakes.

WEEK 3: MEAL PREP GUIDE

Prepping foods on the weekend is a great way to save time during the week. Here are some items you could prep for week 3!

Recipe or Items to Prep	Suggestions	✓ When Completed
Bacon, Tomato & Chive Deviled Eggs (pg. 43)	• Make Deviled Eggs. • Be sure to hard-boil 3 extra eggs for the Salad Nicoise recipe.	
Salad Niçoise (pg. 56)	• Make salad but leave off dressing. • Add dressing just before eating so that romaine stays crisp. • Don't care for tuna – simply add chicken or salmon.	
Italian Burgers (pg. 120)	• Make burgers. • May also use ground chicken or beef. • To make this a quick meal option, grill burgers right away and re-heat before eating OR grill just before serving. • Feel free to double the recipe and freeze the burger patties uncooked for future meals.	
Green Curry Lettuce Wraps (pg. 98)	• Pre-prep as much as you can so that the recipe is simple and quick to put together during the week.	
Chicken Pizzaioli (pg. 109)	• Pre-prep as much as you can so that the recipe is simple and quick to put together during the week.	
Raw Veggies	• Go through the Week 3 meal guide, and wash, prep, and chop all raw veggies so they're ready to be eaten or added to recipes for the week ahead.	
Portion Out Items	• Portion out the following items in bags or individual containers for an easy grab-and-go option. – Almonds (15-20) – Yogurt (1/2-3/4 cup) – Berries (1/2-1 cup) – Side Salads – Deviled Eggs – Cheese or Cottage Cheese	
Optional: Italian Turkey Sausage (pg. 121)	• Make turkey sausage and freeze. • This recipe makes for an easy, tasty and quality protein addition to dishes such as eggs or salads. • *Add ground turkey to grocery list if you choose to make the sausage.*	

Week 4: Lori Harder's Jump Start Meal Guide

"Let food be thy medicine and medicine be thy food." — Hippocrates

WEEK 4	Day 1	Day 2	Day 3	Day 4	Day 5	Day 6	Day 7
Meal 1 *Jump Start Protein Shake recipes on pg. 160-161*	• Meal Replacement Shake OR • Jump Start Protein Shake	• Meal Replacement Shake OR • Jump Start Protein Shake	• Meal Replacement Shake OR • Jump Start Protein Shake	• Meal Replacement Shake OR • Jump Start Protein Shake	• Meal Replacement Shake OR • Jump Start Protein Shake	• Meal Replacement Shake OR • Jump Start Protein Shake	• Meal Replacement Shake OR • Jump Start Protein Shake
Meal 2	**Tomato Cucumber Salad with Feta and Cubed Greek Marinated Chicken Breast** • 1/4 of salad recipe *(see pg. 51)* • 3-5 oz. Cubed Greek-Marinated Chicken Breast *(see pg. 101)* • 1/2-1 cup watermelon	**Lean Mean Green Goulash** • 1 serving (~1/6 of recipe) L/O Lean Mean Green Goulash • 1/2-3/4 cup whole wheat or brown rice pasta *(optional starch)* • 1/2-1 cup fresh berries	**Tomato Cucumber Salad with Feta and Cubed Greek Marinated Chicken Breast** • 1/4 of salad recipe • 3-5 oz. Cubed Greek-Marinated Chicken Breast • 1/2-1 cup watermelon	**Thanksgiving Dinner!** • 3-5 oz. L/O Baked or Grilled Turkey Breast • 2/3-1 cup L/O No Sin Green Bean Casserole • 1/3-2/3 cup L/O Sweet Potato Soufflé	**Tomato Cucumber Salad with Feta and Cubed Greek Marinated Chicken Breast** • 1/4 of salad recipe • 3-5 oz. Cubed Greek-Marinated Chicken Breast • 1/2-1 cup watermelon	**Spinach Artichoke Frittata** • 1/4 of L/O Frittata • Side salad • 1-2 Tbsp. dressing • 1 slice toast *(optional starch)* • 1/2-1 cup berries	L/O Meal Well-balanced! • Protein • Carbs • Healthy Fat

If you prefer, you can enjoy Meal 5 between Meals 1 and 2. Meal 5 is optional and can be consumed whenever you feel you need a little pick-me-up or extra nourishment.

WEEK 4	Day 1	Day 2	Day 3	Day 4	Day 5	Day 6	Day 7
Meal 3 *Jump Start Protein Shake recipes on pg. 160-161*	• Meal Replacement Shake OR • Jump Start Protein Shake OR • Option from Meal Alternative list *(pg. 19)*	• Meal Replacement Shake OR • Jump Start Protein Shake OR • Option from Meal Alternative list *(pg. 19)*	• Meal Replacement Shake OR • Jump Start Protein Shake OR • Option from Meal Alternative list *(pg. 19)*	• Meal Replacement Shake OR • Jump Start Protein Shake OR • Option from Meal Alternative list *(pg. 19)*	• Meal Replacement Shake OR • Jump Start Protein Shake OR • Option from Meal Alternative list *(pg. 19)*	• Meal Replacement Shake OR • Jump Start Protein Shake OR • Option from Meal Alternative list *(pg. 19)*	• Meal Replacement Shake OR • Jump Start Protein Shake OR • Option from Meal Alternative list *(pg. 19)*
Meal 4	**Lean Mean Green Goulash** • 1 serving (~1/6 of recipe) Lean Mean Green Goulash *(see pg. 129)* • 1/2-3/4 cup whole-wheat or brown rice pasta *(optional starch)*	**Go-To Balanced Meal** • 3-5 oz. Meat (grilled, baked, stir fried or sautéed) • 3/4-1½ cup roasted veggies *(Suggestion: See Simple Roasted Vegetables recipe on pg. 84)* • side salad • 1-2 Tbsp. dressing	**Thanksgiving Dinner!** • 3-5 oz. Baked or Grilled Turkey Breast • 2/3-1 cup No Sin Green Bean Casserole *(see pg. 90)* • 1/3-2/3 cup Sweet Potato Soufflé *(see pg. 95)*	**Spinach Artichoke Frittata** • 1/4 of Frittata *(see pg. 32)* • side salad • 1-2 Tbsp. dressing • 1 slice toast *(optional starch)*	**Go-To Balanced Meal** • 3-5 oz. Meat (grill, baked, stir fried or sautéed) • 3/4-1½ cups roasted veggies *(Suggestion: See Simple Roasted Vegetables recipe on pg. 84)* • side salad • 1-2 Tbsp. dressing	**"Freestyle" Salad** • 3-5 oz. L/O chicken/meat/turkey burger served on a bed of greens with chopped veggies of choice • 1-2 Tbsp. chopped nuts • 1-2 Tbsp. cheese • 1-2 Tbsp. dressing • 1 slice of toast *(optional starch)*	**Meal of your choice** • Plan ahead • Use portion control • Enjoy!
Meal 5 *Optional meal – you choose where it fits best*	**Apple Walnut Pancakes** • 1/2-1 serving Apple Walnut Pancake recipe *(see pg. 22)* • 1-1½ Tbsp. nut/seed butter • 1/2-1 cup fresh berries	**On-the-Go Snack** • 3-5 egg whites or 1-2 whole eggs • 15-20 almonds • 1 small apple	**It's Like Dessert!** • 1 slice of Banana Bread *(see pg. 26)* • 1 Tbsp. nut/seed butter	**Apple Walnut Pancakes** • 1/2-1 serving Apple Walnut Pancake recipe • 1-1½ Tbsp. nut/seed butter • 1/2-1 cup fresh berries	**On-the-Go Snack** • 3-5 egg whites or 1-2 whole eggs • 15-20 almonds • 1 small apple	**It's Like Dessert!** • 1 slice of Banana Bread • 1 Tbsp. nut/seed butter	**Apple Walnut Pancakes** • 1/2-1 serving Apple Walnut Pancake recipe • 1-1½ Tbsp. nut/seed butter • 1/2-1 cup fresh berries

L/O = Leftover

Isagenix is Lori's recommended meal replacement shake. For questions regarding Isagenix products, contact Lori at hello@busygirlhealthylife.com.

WEEK 4: GROCERY LIST

1st Day Item Is Needed	Groceries	Quantity	Recommendations/Notes
Produce			
Day 1	Tomatoes	2 medium	For Tomato Cucumber Salad
Day 1	Cucumber	1 medium	For Tomato Cucumber Salad
Day 1	Fresh Basil	6 leaves	For Tomato Cucumber Salad – may have L/O fresh basil from Week 3
Day 1	Green Bell Pepper	1/2	For Lean Mean Green Goulash
Day 1	Red Bell Pepper	1/2	For Lean Mean Green Goulash
Day 1	Onion	3-4	For recipes
Day 1	Zucchini	4 medium	For Lean Mean Green Goulash
Day 2	Salad Greens	1 large bag or container	Add a side salad to any meal! Spring mix, arugula, kale, romaine, etc.
Day 2	Raw Veggies of Choice	Variety	Always keep on hand, washed and pre-chopped for an easy snack and easy add-ins to eggs, salads, for sautéing or roasting.
Day 3	Sliced Mushrooms	8 oz. fresh	For No Sin Green Bean Casserole
Day 3	Green Beans (frozen)	2 (16 oz.) bag	For No Sin Green Bean Casserole
Day 4	Spinach (frozen)	1 (8 oz.) bag	For Spinach Artichoke Frittata
Day 3	Sweet Potato	6	For Sweet Potato Soufflé
Day 1	Lemon	1	For Tomato Cucumber Salad
Day 1	Watermelon	3 cups	Can purchase already cubed for an easy option.
Day 1	Apples	4 medium	For Apple Walnut Pancakes and snacks
Day 2	Berries	2 (6 oz.) containers	Fresh or frozen. If frozen make sure there aren't any added sugars.
Day 3	Banana	3 medium	For Banana Bread. Best if very ripe.
Protein/Dairy			
Day 1	Eggs	3 dozen	Organic/pasture-raised is best — high in Omega 3s & fatty acids. For pancakes, banana bread, hard-boiled eggs, Sweet Potato Soufflé, and Spinach Artichoke Frittata.
Day 1	Chicken Breast	1 lb.	For Greek-Marinated Chicken Breast. <90 mg sodium/serving
Day 1	Lean Ground Beef	1 lb.	For Lean Mean Green Goulash
Day 2	Meat of Choice	2 lbs.	Suggestions: Wild-caught fish, pork loin, chicken, sirloin or filet.
Day 3	Turkey Breast	1 lb.	If preferred, you could purchase a whole turkey and free leftovers.
Day 1	Feta Cheese	1/2 cup	For Tomato Cucumber Salad
Day 1	Cottage Cheese	1 cup	Suggested Brand: Kalona Super Natural or Organic Valley if available. For Apple Walnut Pancakes and Spinach Artichoke Frittata
Day 3	Buttermilk	2 cups	For No Sin Green Bean Casserole and Sweet Potato Soufflé
Day 3	Parmesan	2 Tbsp.	For No Sin Green Bean Casserole
Day 3	Butter	3 Tbsp.	For Sweet Potato Soufflé
Day 4	Laughing Cow Swiss Cheese	3 wedges	For Spinach Artichoke Frittata. Could also use 1/4 cup leftover cheese from Week 1.
Breads/Grains			
Day 1	Pasta	1 small box	Optional starch to go with Lean Mean Green Goulash. Recommend: whole-wheat, rice or quinoa pasta
Day 1	Oats	1/2-1 cup	For Apple Walnut Pancakes
Day 4	Bread	1 bag	For optional starch. Recommend: Sprouted Grain Bread (Ezekiel) or Gluten-Free bread. Store in freezer.
Day 3	Whole-Wheat Pastry Flour	1¼ cup	For Banana Bread and No Sin Green Bean Casserole. Can purchase in bulk at a co-op.
Dry/Canned Goods			
Day 1	Kalamata Olives	2 Tbsp.	For Greek Marinated Chicken Breast. May have L/Os from previous week.
Day 1	Whole Tomatoes	1 (14 oz.) can	For Lean Mean Green Goulash
Day 1	Tomato Paste	1 small can	For Lean Mean Green Goulash – Freeze L/O paste for future recipes.
Day 1	Chopped Walnuts	1/4 cup	For Apple Walnut Pancakes
Day 3	Water Chestnuts	1 (8 oz.) can	For No Sin Green Bean Casserole
Day 3	Dry White Wine	1/2 cup	For No Sin Green Bean Casserole – Can substitute chicken broth/stock.
Day 3	Sliced or Slivered Almonds	1/2 cup	For No Sin Green Bean Casserole
Day 3	Chopped Pecans	1/4 cup	For Sweet Potato Soufflé
Day 3	Applesauce	3/4 cup	For Banana Bread – no sugar added
Day 4	Marinated Artichoke Hearts	1 (9 oz.) jar	For Spinach Artichoke Frittata

*   If cooking for others, you may need to adjust quantities.
** If not using a meal replacement shake for Meals 1 and 3, you will need to add those ingredients to your list for snacks and morning shakes.

WEEK 4: MEAL PREP GUIDE

Prepping foods on the weekend is a great way to save time during the week. Here are some items you could prep for week 4!

Recipe or Items to Prep	Suggestions	✓ When Completed
Tomato Cucumber Salad (pg. 51)	• Make salad for the week ahead.	
Greek-Marinated Chicken Breast (pg. 101)	• Marinate and bake chicken. • Allow to cool then cube and add to Tomato Cucumber Salad.	
Apple Walnut Pancakes (pg. 22)	• Make 2 servings of Apple Walnut Pancakes. • Feel free to make more and freeze for future meal preps or for a quick grab-and-go snack.	
Banana Bread (pg. 26)	• Make Banana Bread and store in refrigerator. • Could also freeze half of batch for future meal preps.	
Lean Mean Green Goulash (pg. 129)	• To make this a quick meal option, you can prepare the entire meal and re-heat OR prep and chop all of the ingredients so that you can have this dish on the table in no time. • Freezer-friendly meal. Freeze in single servings if you have more L/Os than you need.	
No-Sin Green Bean Casserole (pg. 90)	• To make this a quick meal option, you can prepare the entire meal and re-heat OR prep and combine all of the ingredients and bake just before serving. • Freezer-friendly dish. Freeze in single servings if you have more L/Os than you need.	
Sweet Potato Soufflé (pg. 95)	• To make this a quick meal option, you can prepare the entire meal and re-heat OR prep and combine all of the ingredients and bake just before serving. • Freezer friendly.	
Hard-Boiled Eggs	• Hard-boil 6-12 eggs for the week ahead.	
Raw Veggies	• Go through the Week 4 meal guide, and wash, prep, and chop all raw veggies so that they're ready to be eaten or added to recipes for the week ahead.	
Portion Out Items	• Portion out the following items in bags or individual containers for easy grab and go. – Almonds (15-20) – Hard-Boiled Eggs – Berries (1/2-1 cup) – Side Salads – Pancakes – Banana Bread	
Optional: Italian Turkey Sausage (pg. 121)	• Make turkey sausage and freeze. • This recipe makes for an easy, tasty and quality protein addition to dishes such as eggs or salads. • *Add ground turkey to grocery list if you choose to make the sausage.*	

MEAL ALTERNATIVES

Short on time? Not diggin' the meal listed on the meal guide? That's why this list was created! This list includes several options that you can choose from to substitute any meal on the meal guide. The key is to make a healthy and well-balanced meal — making sure each meal includes a quality source of protein.

Meal 3 Alternatives
• Protein Shake (see recipe options on pg. 160-161)
Yogurt/Cottage Cheese Parfait   • 1/2–1 cup Plain Greek Yogurt **OR** Cottage Cheese   • 1/4–1/2 cup Berries **OR** 1 Fruit of Choice   • 1–2 Tbsp. Chopped Nuts **OR** Small Handful of Nuts (almonds, walnuts, pecans etc.) **OR** 1–2 Tbsp. Nut Butter
• 1/2–1 cup Cottage Cheese or 1 oz. of Cheese of Choice   • Raw Veggies with 3–4 Tbsp. Hummus   • 1 Fruit of Choice
• 1–2 Hard-Boiled Eggs **OR** 3–4 Hard-Boiled Egg Whites   **OR** 1–2 Breakfast Biscuits (see pg. 25)   • 1 Fruit of Choice
• 1–2 Hard-Boiled Eggs **OR** 3–4 Hard-Boiled Egg Whites   • 1 Fruit of Choice   • Small Handful of Nuts (almonds, walnuts, pecans etc.)
Open-Faced Avocado Egg Sandwich   • 1–2 Hard-Boiled Eggs **OR** 3–4 Hard-Boiled Egg Whites   • 1 Slice Sprouted-Grain **OR** Gluten-Free Bread   • 1/4 Sliced Avocado   • 1/4–3/4 cup Berries
• 1–2 Protein Pancakes (see recipes on pg. 22)   • Small Handful of Nuts (almonds, walnuts, pecans etc.) **OR** 1–2 Tbsp. Nut Butter
• 3–5 No-Bake PB Pumpkin Balls (see recipe on pg. 149)   • 1/2–1 cup Cottage Cheese **OR** 1–2 Hard-Boiled Eggs **OR** 3–4 Hard-Boiled Egg Whites
• 1 Fruit of Choice   • 3–4 Tbsp. Awesomely Autumn Pumpkin Dip (see recipe on pg. 150)   • Small Handful of Nuts (almonds, walnuts, pecans etc.)
Lower-Carb Meal Options
• *2–4 Breakfast Biscuits (see pg. 25)*   • *Small Handful of Nuts (almonds, walnuts, pecans etc.)*
• *1–2 Hard-Boiled Eggs OR 3–4 Hard-Boiled Egg Whites*   • *Raw Veggies with 3–4 Tbsp. Hummus*
• *1/2–1 cup Cottage Cheese or 1 oz. of Cheese of Choice*   • *Raw Veggies with 3–4 Tbsp. Hummus*
• *2–4 Breakfast Biscuits (see pg. 25)*   • *Raw Veggies with 3–4 Tbsp. Hummus*

WHY SUPPLEMENTATION?

By now, you're aware that the meal plan includes meal replacements. Isagenix® is Lori's supplement of choice, however you may have a favorite brand or type that works for you. If you choose not to use meal supplements, refer to the meal alternatives list on page 19. Listed below are reasons why supplementation is a great idea (in addition to wholesome and healthy meals).

* Quick, healthy and portable meal options for busy lifestyles — when time is not in your favor.

* Cuts down on the amount of time you spend in the kitchen meal prepping.

* High-quality and easily absorbable nutrition.

* Great option for post-workout meals that promote quick recovery.

* Saves time and eliminates temptations for fast-food meals or skipping meals.

What to look for?
* Contains high-quality, natural ingredients

* No artificial ingredients including colors, flavorings and sweeteners (e.g., sucralose, aspartame)

* Doesn't contain soy as the main source of protein

* It contains a high-quality, undenatured whey protein

* If you follow a dairy-free diet, look for an alternative soy-free protein product such as rice, hemp seed, pea etc.

Why Lori chooses Isagenix
These products are perfect for the person on the go! IsaLean® Shakes are a quick meal replacement that keeps you full, satisfied and on track with your goals. Curb cravings and build lean muscle with an easy delicious shake!

The IsaLean Shakes are nutritionally balanced so you don't have to plan out every meal. Simply replace 2–3 of your meals a day with Isagenix IsaLean Shakes or IsaLean® Bars.

* Undenatured whey protein from grass-fed organically raised cows
  — Undenatured = whey protein in its most natural form, which is highly absorbable.

* No soy

* No artificial ingredients including sweeteners, flavors and colorings

* Non-GMO

* Gluten free

* Dairy-free option available (vegan friendly)

If interested in incorporating and learning more about Isagenix, please send an email to hello@busygirlhealthylife.com and include a phone number to be reached at.

breakfast

apple walnut pancakes

Makes 2 servings.

INGREDIENTS

- 4 egg whites
- ½ c. oatmeal
- ¼ c. cottage cheese
- 3 packets stevia or natural sweetener of choice
- 1 apple diced
- 2 Tbsp. chopped walnuts
- 1 tsp. cinnamon

INSTRUCTIONS

1. Combine all ingredients in food processor or blender. Blend until smooth. Spray frying pan with a nonstick spray. Pour batter into frying pan and cook on med/low heat until golden brown on each side.

Nutritional Value
Nutritional information is based on 1/2 of the recipe.

Calories: 210 ❀ Fat: 7g ❀ Sodium: 225mg ❀ Carbohydrates: 24g ❀ Fiber: 25g ❀ Sugar: 8g ❀ Protein: 15g

banana nut pancakes

Makes 2 servings.

INGREDIENTS

- 4 egg whites
- ½ c. oatmeal
- ¼ c. cottage cheese
- 3 packets stevia or natural sweetener of choice
- ½ banana
- 2 Tbsp. walnuts
- 1 tsp. cinnamon

INSTRUCTIONS

1. Combine all ingredients in food processor or blender. Blend until smooth. Spray frying pan with a nonstick spray. Pour batter into frying pan and cook on med/low heat until golden brown on each side.

Nutritional Value
Nutritional information is based on 1/2 of the recipe.

Calories: 210 ❀ Fat: 7g ❀ Sodium: 225mg ❀ Carbohydrates: 24g ❀ Fiber: 4g ❀ Sugar: 6g ❀ Protein: 15g

banana oatmeal

Makes 1 serving.

INGREDIENTS

¼ cup oatmeal

1 Tbsp. chia seeds

1 tsp. coconut oil

cinnamon to taste

1 tsp. maple syrup

½ banana

Submitted
by
Angela Schwartz
of Minnesota

INSTRUCTIONS

1. Make oatmeal per package directions.

2. Add chia seeds and coconut oil, and stir until coconut oil melts.

3. Let sit for a minute to allow the seeds to soak up some water.

4. Add cinnamon to taste and stir.

5. Cut banana into slices to the oatmeal.

6. Top with maple syrup.

Nutritional Value
Nutritional information is based on 1 serving.

Calories: 225 ✷ Fat: 9g ✷ Carbohydrates: 38g ✷ Fiber: 9g ✷ Protein: 6g ✷ Sugar: 13g

banana french toast sticks

Makes 2 servings (serving = about 5 sticks).

INGREDIENTS

3	slices Ezekiel® bread (or bread of your choice)
1	egg
1	egg white
1	tsp. vanilla
5	packets stevia or 3 Tbsp. sugar
3	Tbsp. low-fat buttermilk
½	banana
½	tsp. cinnamon

INSTRUCTIONS

1. Preheat oven to 375 degrees.
2. Cut each slice of bread in 3 to 4 strips and set aside.
3. Add the remaining ingredients in a food processor or blender. Blend until smooth.
4. Soak the strips of bread in the mixture until completely soaked.
5. Spray a baking sheet with nonstick spray and place saturated sticks on pan.
6. Bake for 15 to 20 minutes depending on the desired level of crunch. Flip the sticks halfway through baking so they are golden brown on each side.
7. Sprinkle with cinnamon and/or stevia (or any other natural sweetener) or your favorite topping such as powdered sugar, low-sugar syrup, jam, etc.

> *"I thought of this recipe out of the blue one day just messing around in the kitchen while my husband watched football. My fridge was almost empty and we were having some serious French toast cravings, and this is what I came up with! I think the Ezekiel bread really adds some heartiness and flavor to it."*

Nutritional Value
Nutritional information is based on 1 serving.

Calories: 195   Fat: 1g   Carbohydrates: 30g   Protein: 13g   Sugar: 5g

breakfast biscuits

Makes 24 mini biscuits.

INGREDIENTS

5	egg whites
1	egg
¼	c. low-fat buttermilk
½	c. fat-free cottage cheese
1	c. low-fat, shredded sharp cheddar cheese
6	oz. (11 slices) turkey bacon, diced
½	c. diced sweet onion
1	c. Whole-Wheat Bread Crumbs, pg. 163
½	tsp. olive oil
¾	tsp. garlic powder
¼	tsp. red pepper flakes
	dash of nutmeg

INSTRUCTIONS

1. Preheat oven to 375 degrees.

2. Heat olive oil in frying pan. Add diced turkey bacon and cook on medium-high until almost crisp.

3. Add diced onions and sauté until onions are opaque. Let cool.

4. Beat egg whites, egg, buttermilk, garlic powder, red pepper flakes and nutmeg in a large mixing bowl.

5. Add cheddar cheese, cottage cheese, turkey bacon, onion and bread crumbs to egg mixture. Salt and pepper to taste, and mix all ingredients well.

6. Spray mini muffin pan with olive oil spray. Fill muffin cups to top, sprinkle lightly with paprika.

7. Bake for 12 to 15 minutes. Remove muffins from pan and let stand for 10 minutes.

"This is definitely a great grab-and-go meal! I love to keep them in the freezer and warm them up when I am in the mood for a warm breakfast in a hurry."

Nutritional Value
Nutritional information is based on 1 biscuit.

Calories: 46   Fat: 2g   Carbohydrates: 3g   Protein: 5g   Sugar: <1g

banana bread

Makes 8 large slices.

INGREDIENTS

1½	c. whole-wheat pastry flour
2	tsp. baking powder
½	tsp. salt
12	packets stevia or ½ c. sugar
2	Tbsp. cocoa powder
1	egg plus 2 egg whites
1	c. mashed ripe bananas
¾	c. applesauce
1	tsp. vanilla extract

INSTRUCTIONS

1. Preheat oven to 350 degrees.

2. In large mixing bowl, combine all dry ingredients.
   In medium mixing bowl combine all wet ingredients and mix
   well. Add wet mixture to dry mixture and stir until just blended.

3. Spoon batter into a large loaf pan (9" x 5") coated with nonstick spray.

4. Bake for 45 to 50 minutes until knife inserted in middle comes out clean.

> "Some of my favorite memories are coming home from school and having the house smell like my mom's banana bread. There is something so comforting about having a slice of this old-fashioned favorite. If I'm really in the mood to get crazy and have a healthy indulgence, I throw a few dark chocolate chips on top!"

Nutritional Value
Nutritional information is based on 1 slice.

Calories: 125 ✿ Fat: 1g ✿ Carbohydrates: 22g ✿ Protein: 5g ✿ Sugar: 6g

buttermilk sausage gravy & biscuits

Makes 8 servings.

INGREDIENTS

1¼ c. Italian Turkey Sausage, *pg. 121*

3 Tbsp. whole-wheat flour

1½ c. low-sodium chicken stock

1½ c. low-fat buttermilk

dash of ground nutmeg

8 whole-grain, light English muffins (split and lightly toasted)

salt and pepper to taste

INSTRUCTIONS

1. Heat up the sausage in a nonstick cooking pan.

2. Add flour and heat for 1 to 2 minutes more.

3. Add chicken stock, buttermilk and nutmeg, and bring to a soft simmer on medium-high heat stirring constantly until mixture thickens (about 5 minutes).

4. Put ¼ cup of sausage gravy on each half of English muffin. Serve immediately.

Nutritional Value
Nutritional information is based on 1 serving.

Calories: 167 ❄ Fat: 3g ❄ Carbohydrates: 21g ❄ Protein: 12g ❄ Sugar: 4g

pick your patty - breakfast sandwich

Makes 4 egg patties and 18 sausage patties.

INGREDIENTS

Sausage Patty

2	lbs. ground turkey
1	c. oatmeal
3	egg whites
1½	tsp. red pepper flakes
2	tsp. Italian seasoning
2½	tsp. fennel seed
1	tsp. cayenne pepper
1	tsp. garlic powder
3	packets stevia or 2 Tbsp. sugar

Thoroughly mix all ingredients. Make 18 (¾-inch) patties.
Fry in a nonstick frying pan until cooked through.
Makes 18 turkey sausage patties.

Egg and Cheese Patty

6	egg whites
1	Tbsp. skim milk
¼	c. reduced-fat shredded sharp cheddar cheese
	pinch of dried thyme leaves
	dash of hot sauce

Beat all ingredients together. Pour in sprayed frying pan and cook until eggs are set,
flipping half-way through. Divide into 4 pieces. Makes 4 egg patties.

INSTRUCTIONS

1. Toast whole-grain English muffin. Add one sausage patty and one egg cheese patty between
   muffin for a delicious, healthy and filling breakfast sandwich for under 300 calories.

Nutritional Value

1 Sausage Patty
Calories: 93 ❀ Fat: 4g ❀ Carbohydrates: 2g ❀ Protein: 11g ❀ Sugar: 0g

1 Egg and Cheese Patty
Calories: 51 ❀ Fat: 2g ❀ Carbohydrates: 1g ❀ Protein: 8g ❀ Sugar: 1g

sausage egg & cheese breakfast sandwich

Makes 10 sandwiches.

INGREDIENTS

- 1 lb. ground turkey (93/7)
- 2 tsp. olive oil
- ½ tsp. each of garlic powder, red pepper flakes and paprika
- 1 tsp. each Italian seasoning and dried fennel seed
- ¼ tsp. cayenne pepper
- salt and pepper to taste
- 2 eggs
- 8 egg whites
- 10 low-fat cheese slices
- 10 light, whole-grain English muffins (split and lightly toasted)

INSTRUCTIONS

1. Preheat oven to 350 degrees.

2. Beat eggs and egg whites together and pour into a pre-sprayed 9x11 baking dish. Bake in oven for 12 minutes or until eggs are set and cooked through. Cut cooked eggs into 10 pieces.

3. Add all spices to ground turkey and mix well with hands until spices are evenly distributed.

4. Divide turkey into 10 pieces and make them into thin patties. Fry sausage patties in a nonstick frying pan until patties are cooked thoroughly.

5. Put 1 sausage patty, 1 egg patty and 1 slice of cheese on a lightly toasted English muffin and enjoy! It tastes great with a little dijon mustard on the sandwich.

tip:

Freezes well. Make all 10 sandwiches and freeze. To reheat, just wrap frozen sandwich in paper towel and microwave on high for to 1½ minutes.

Nutritional Value
Nutritional information is based on 1 sandwich.

Calories: 246   Fat: 8g   Carbohydrates: 20g   Protein: 21g   Sugar: 2g

mango cream muffins

Makes 12 muffins.

INGREDIENTS

1¼ c. whole-wheat pastry flour

⅔ c. oat flour

1½ tsp. baking powder

½ tsp. baking soda

¼ tsp. salt

1 c. fat-free sour cream or fat-free Greek yogurt

3 Tbsp. light butter, melted

1 tsp. vanilla

2 egg whites, beaten

½ c. low-fat buttermilk

2 c. diced frozen mangos, thawed

12 packets stevia or ½ c. sugar

INSTRUCTIONS

1. Preheat oven to 400 degrees.

2. Mix all dry ingredients together in a mixing bowl.

3. Then in a separate bowl, mix all wet ingredients together.

4. Combine wet and dry ingredients and stir until mostly smooth, some small lumps are ok.

5. Spray muffin pan (12 count) with cooking spray. Fill muffin cups almost to top and bake for 25 minutes or until cooked through.

6. Try the toothpick trick! Insert toothpick. If it comes out clean, muffins are done.

> *"A healthy life is all about balance, and I believe you should be able to eat dessert a few times a week using portion control. Small servings of the healthier options keep this busy girl sane!"*

Nutritional Value

Nutritional information is based on 1 muffin.

Calories: 132 ❀ Fat: 2g ❀ Carbohydrates: 23g ❀ Protein: 8g ❀ Sugar: 5g

breakfast burrito

Makes 8 burritos.

INGREDIENTS

- 10   egg whites
- 2   eggs
- ¼   c. skim milk
- ¼   tsp. ground cumin
- ½   c. diced red pepper
- ½   c. diced green pepper
- ¾   c. diced onion
- 1   finely diced garlic clove
- ¾   c. fat-free cottage cheese
- 1   c. cooked turkey sausage
- ½   c. black beans, drained and rinsed (optional)
-    salt and pepper to taste
- 8   whole-wheat 6-inch tortilla shells

INSTRUCTIONS

1. Beat together egg whites, eggs, skim milk and cumin.
2. Mix in cottage cheese, salt and pepper to taste.
3. Sauté onions and peppers until onions are opaque.
4. Add garlic and cook for one minute more.
5. Remove from pan, add egg mixture to pan and scramble eggs on medium-low heat until almost set.
6. Add peppers and onions to egg mixture.
7. Add cooked turkey sausage and black beans, and mix together.
8. Put ½ c. of egg mixture into a warm whole-wheat tortilla shell, garnish with diced fresh tomatoes and roll into burrito. May garnish with 1 Tbsp. of your favorite salsa for extra spice.

hint:

Store cooked egg mixture in the refrigerator. For a quick breakfast on the go, just put ½ c. of filling in tortilla shell, garnish with fresh diced tomato and microwave for one minute.

Nutritional Value

Nutritional information is based on ½ c. egg serving with 1 whole-wheat tortilla shell.

Calories: 144   Fat: 5g   Carbohydrates: 15g   Protein: 20g   Sugar: 2g

spinach artichoke frittata

Makes 4 generous servings.

INGREDIENTS

8 oz. frozen chopped spinach,
thawed and water squeezed out

9 oz. jar marinated artichoke hearts,
drained and chopped

¾ to 1 c. chopped sweet onions
pinch of red pepper flakes

½ c. fat-free cottage cheese

3 wedges Laughing Cow® Light Swiss Cheese

8 egg whites

2 eggs

¼ tsp. garlic powder
splash of water
pinch of nutmeg

INSTRUCTIONS

1. Preheat oven to 350 degrees.

2. Generously spray frying pan with cooking spray. Sauté spinach, onion, artichoke
   and red pepper flakes until onion is tender. Add cottage cheese, Laughing Cow
   and cook until cheese melts.

3. Beat egg whites, eggs and garlic powder with a splash of water.

4. Add to spinach and cheese mixture. Cook for 2 minutes.

5. Place the mixture into a 10- to 12-inch baking dish. Sprinkle top with a pinch of
   nutmeg and bake for 20 minutes or until frittata is set. Remove from oven and
   let stand for 5 to 10 minutes.

Leftovers are great reheated!

Nutritional Value

Nutritional information is based on about ¼ of dish.

Calories: 196 ❁ Fat: 8g ❁ Carbohydrates: 12g ❁ Protein: 18g ❁ Sugar: 4g

broccoli mushroom onion frittata

Makes 4 generous servings.

INGREDIENTS

1½	c. chopped broccoli
1	4 oz. can mushrooms, drained and diced
¾	to 1 c. diced sweet onion
½	c. fat-free cottage cheese
3	wedges Laughing Cow® Light Swiss Cheese
8	egg whites
2	eggs
	splash of water
½	tsp. garlic powder
	pinch of red pepper flakes
⅛	tsp. dried thyme leaves

INSTRUCTIONS

1. Preheat oven to 350 degrees.

2. Generously spray frying pan with cooking spray. Sauté broccoli, mushrooms, onion and red pepper flakes until tender. Add cottage cheese, Laughing Cow and cook until cheese melts.

3. Beat egg whites, eggs and garlic powder with a splash of water.

4. Add to broccoli and cheese mixture. Cook for 2 minutes.

5. Place the mixture into a 10- to 12-inch baking dish. Bake for 20 minutes or until frittata is set. Remove from oven and let stand for 5 to 10 minutes.

Leftovers are great reheated!

Nutritional Value

Nutritional information is based on about ¼ of dish.

Calories: 154   Fat: 3g   Carbohydrates: 8g   Protein: 18g   Sugar: 5g

appetizers

cheesy broccoli bites

Makes about 36 bites.

INGREDIENTS

16	oz. organic frozen broccoli florets, thawed
½	c. shredded low-fat sharp cheddar cheese
2	uncooked turkey sausages, outer skins removed
1	egg white
2	Tbsp. Whole-Wheat Bread Crumbs, *see pg. 163*
1	tsp. garlic powder
	salt and pepper to taste

INSTRUCTIONS

1. Preheat oven to 375 degrees.

2. Pat broccoli florets dry with paper toweling. Put broccoli in food processor and pulse until finely chopped. Add cheese, sausage, egg white, bread crumbs and garlic powder and pulse until blended.

3. Transfer broccoli mixture to bowl and scoop out with a teaspoon and roll into walnut-sized balls.

4. Put on baking sheet and bake for 25 minutes or until sausage is thoroughly cooked.

5. Serve with ranch dressing on the side.

Nutritional Value
Nutritional information is based on 1 broccoli bite (ranch dressing not included).

Calories: 16   Fat: 1g   Sodium: 65mg   Carbohydrates: 1g   Fiber: .5g   Sugar: 0g   Protein: 1g

caramelized onion dip

Makes about 8 servings.

INGREDIENTS

2	c. sweet onion (such as walla walla), finely diced
1	6 oz. container of fat-free Greek yogurt
¼	c. low-fat ricotta cheese
2	Tbsp. grated Parmesan cheese
1	tsp. olive oil
2	tsp. good balsamic vinegar
½	tsp. garlic powder
1-2	Tbsp. chopped fresh chives
	salt and pepper to taste

INSTRUCTIONS

1. Spray nonstick spray in a nonstick pan.

2. Sauté onions on medium-low until caramelized to a golden-light brown and tender (about 20-30 minutes). Can add a little water if onions start to stick to pan.

3. While onions are sautéing, add remaining ingredients, except chives, in a medium-sized bowl and mix well.

4. When onions are done, remove from heat and let cool.

5. Add onions and chives to the mixture and gently mix together.

6. Salt and pepper to taste. If dip is too thick, add a tablespoon or so of water until you reach desired consistency.

7. Let dip set in refrigerator for a hour or two for flavors to blend. Remove from refrigerator about 45 minutes before serving.

note:

Dip is great with veggies, crackers, toasted baguettes etc. Would also be delicious on a baked potato instead of sour cream.

Nutritional Value
Nutritional information is based on 1/4 cup.

Calories: 50   Fat: 1g   Sodium: 160mg   Carbohydrates: 6g   Fiber: 1g   Sugar: 3g   Protein: 5g

buffalo chicken dip

Makes about 12 servings.

INGREDIENTS

⅔ c. fat-free or low-fat Greek yogurt

⅓–½ c. Franks® Hot Sauce or Sriracha sauce

½ c. crumbled light blue cheese

1 tsp. white wine vinegar

1 Tbsp. coconut sugar

2 c. (14 oz.) cooked shredded chicken

½-1 tsp. liquid smoke

¼ c. ranch dressing

⅔ c. celery, finely diced

INSTRUCTIONS

1. Mix all ingredients in a slow cooker, and cook on Low for 3-4 hours or simmer on the stove top for a half hour.

2. Serve with veggies, crackers, baguettes etc.

Nutritional Value
Nutritional information is based on 1/4 cup.

Calories: 90 ⬤ Fat: 3g ⬤ Sodium: 400mg ⬤ Carbohydrates: 2g ⬤ Fiber: 0g ⬤ Sugar: 2g ⬤ Protein: 13g

crab artichoke dip

Makes about 12 servings.

INGREDIENTS

- 14 oz. can artichoke hearts, drained and finely chopped
- 1⅓ c. lump crab meat (about 12 oz.)
- ¼ c. red bell pepper, finely diced
- ¼ c. sweet onion, finely diced
- ¼ tsp. red pepper flakes
- ⅓ c. low-fat mayo
- ⅓ c. fat-free or low-fat plain Greek yogurt
- 1 tsp. garlic powder
- ½ c. shredded parmesan
- ½ c. low-fat mozzarella or light swiss cheese

INSTRUCTIONS

1. Mix all ingredients together and put into a baking dish. Bake for 30-35 minutes until bubbly.

2. Remove from oven and let sit for 10 minutes.

3. Serve with crackers, garlic bread or veggies of choice.

Nutritional Value
Nutritional information is based on 1/4 cup.

Calories: 80   Fat: 3g   Sodium:300mg   Carbohydrates: 4g   Fiber: 1g   Sugar: 2g   Protein: 8g

prosciutto-wrapped pears

Makes about 24 appetizers.

INGREDIENTS

2   ripe pears

2   oz. goat cheese

2   tsp. honey

3   oz. prosciutto, sliced into long strips

    lemon juice

    romaine lettuce leaf for garnish

INSTRUCTIONS

1. Blend softened goat cheese with the honey and set aside.

2. Slice pears in half and core. Further slice the pear into 1/4-inch slices. Cover each slice with lemon juice to avoid turning brown.

3. Spread goat cheese over each slice and wrap in prosciutto.

4. Place prosciutto-wrapped pear slices on a romaine lettuce leaf.

5. You may want to further garnish the serving tray with a few walnuts or dried cranberries.

Nutritional Value
Nutritional information is based on 1 appetizer.

Calories: 25   Fat: 1g   Sodium: 90mg   Carbohydrates: 3g   Fiber: 1g   Sugar: 3g   Protein: 5g

roasted cauliflower bites

Makes about 8 servings.

INGREDIENTS

1   small/medium head fresh cauliflower
3   egg whites (beaten)
2   Tbsp. low-fat buttermilk
2   Tbsp. flour
¾   c. panko plain bread crumbs
½   c. grated Parmesan cheese
1   tsp. garlic powder
    salt and pepper to taste

INSTRUCTIONS

1. Preheat oven to 425 degrees.

2. Cut cauliflower into florets. Put cauliflower into bag, add flour and shake until florets are coated.

3. In a bowl, mix bread crumbs, Parmesan and garlic powder together.

4. In a small bowl, beat egg whites and buttermilk together. Remove florets from bag, dip in egg whites and dredge through bread crumb mixture.

5. Put florets on sprayed baking sheet and bake for 20-30 minutes or until tender crisp and lightly brown. Salt and pepper to taste.

6. Serve with ranch dressing on the side. YUM YUM!

Nutritional Value
Nutritional information is based on 1/2 cup.

Calories: 90   Fat: 2g   Sodium: 225mg   Carbohydrates: 13g   Fiber: 2g   Sugar: 3g   Protein: 6g

smokey salmon potato chips

Makes about 30 slices.

INGREDIENTS

3	medium Yukon gold potatoes
4	oz. light cream cheese
4	oz. fat-free Greek yogurt
1	tsp. dried dill weed
½	tsp. garlic salt
6	oz. smoked salmon, finely sliced
	organic olive oil spray
	cayenne pepper
	salt

INSTRUCTIONS

1. Cut potatoes into ⅛- to ¼-inch slices using a mandolin. Spray baking sheet with olive oil spray.

2. Spread potato slices flat on baking sheet and sprinkle lightly with cayenne pepper.

3. Bake until potato chips are crispy (about 20 minutes, depending on thickness of slices) turning halfway through. Remove from oven and allow potato chips to cool.

4. While baking, mix together room-temperature yogurt, cream cheese, dill weed and garlic salt. Then, cut salmon into bite-sized pieces.

5. When chips are cool, spread tops with cream cheese mixture and add salmon to the tops. Serve and enjoy.

tip:
Can also use sweet potatoes instead of Yukon gold potatoes!

Nutritional Value
Nutritional information is based on 1 slice.

Calories: 30   Fat: 1g   Sodium: 100mg   Carbohydrates: 3g   Fiber: 0g   Sugar: 1g   Protein: 2g

sausage mushroom tartlets

Makes 15 tartlets.

INGREDIENTS

- 1½ c. finely diced portobello mushrooms
- ¼ c. each of finely diced celery and water chestnuts
- 2 Tbsp. finely diced onion
- ½ c. Italian Turkey Sausage, *pg. 121*
- 3 oz. fat-free cream cheese, room temperature
- 1 box (15 count) mini phyllo cups
- salt and pepper to taste

INSTRUCTIONS

1. Preheat oven to 375 degrees.

2. Put finely diced mushroom, celery, water chestnuts and onion in microwave-safe bowl. Microwave on high for one minute.

3. Add cream cheese and sausage to hot mixture. Mix well until cream cheese is melted.

4. Fill mini phyllo cups with mixture.

5. Bake in oven for 12 to 15 minutes.

Nutritional Value
Nutritional information is based on 1 tartlet.

Calories: 32   Fat: 1g   Carbohydrates: 4g   Protein: 3g   Sugar: <1g

bacon, tomato and chive deviled eggs

Makes 12 deviled eggs.

INGREDIENTS

6	hard-boiled eggs (discard 3 of the yolks)
3	Tbsp. fat-free Greek yogurt
1	Tbsp. low-fat mayo
1	tsp. dijon mustard
1	packet stevia or 2 tsp. sugar
1	Tbsp. finely chopped chives
	paprika
¼	tsp. onion powder
¼	tsp. garlic powder
⅛	tsp. red pepper flakes
4-5	strips cooked turkey bacon
3	Tbsp. finely chopped tomatoes (optional)

INSTRUCTIONS

1. Cut eggs in half lengthwise.
2. Discard three of the yolks; put the other three yolks in a bowl with the yogurt, mayo, mustard and sweetener.
3. Mash yolks and mix ingredients well.
4. Add the onion powder, garlic powder and red pepper flakes. Mix well.
5. Stir in the tomatoes and bacon, salt and pepper to taste.
6. Fill the egg whites with the mixture. Lightly sprinkle with paprika and top the eggs with the chives.
7. Chill for about an hour.

tip:

For the perfect hard-boiled egg, cover eggs with cold water and heat on high uncovered until water comes to a rolling boil. Take eggs off the heat and let sit covered for 20 minutes. Then, drain eggs and put in cold water until cooled. Eggs peel easily and no more dark color around the yolk!

Nutritional Value
Nutritional information based on 1 deviled egg.

Calories: 32   Fat: 4g   Carbohydrates: <1g   Protein: 2g   Sugar: <1g

crab tartlets

Makes 15 tartlets.

INGREDIENTS

- ⅓ c. each finely diced celery and sweet red pepper
- 2 Tbsp. finely diced onion
- 4 oz. diced imitation crab (can use real crab or shrimp)
- ¼ tsp. garlic powder
- 3 oz. fat-free cream cheese, room temperature
- 1 Tbsp. low-fat mayo or fat-free Greek yogurt
- 1 box (15 count) mini phyllo cups
  salt and pepper to taste

INSTRUCTIONS

1. Preheat oven to 375 degrees.
2. Put finely diced pepper, celery and onion in microwave-safe bowl. Microwave on high for 1 minute.
3. Add cream cheese, mayo, garlic powder and crab to hot mixture. Mix well until cream cheese is melted.
4. Fill mini phyllo cups with mixture.
5. Bake in oven for 12 to 15 minutes.

Nutritional Value
Nutritional information based on 1 tartlet.

Calories: 29   Fat: 1g   Carbohydrates: 4g   Protein: 2g   Sugar: <1g

hot banana pepper goat cheese boats

Makes 16 boats.

INGREDIENTS

8   banana peppers (about 4 inches long each)
8   tsp. goat cheese

INSTRUCTIONS

1.   Preheat oven to 450 degrees.

2.   Slice peppers in half lengthwise. Remove seeds.

3.   Bake in hot oven for 3 to 4 minutes until peppers are cooked, but still firm.

4.   Remove from oven and let cool.

5.   Spread ½ tsp. of goat cheese on each pepper half.

Nutritional Value
Nutritional information based on 1 boat.

Calories: 8   Fat: <1g   Carbohydrates: <1g   Protein: <1g   Sugar: 0g

asian meatballs

Makes 40 meatballs.

INGREDIENTS

1½	lbs. ground turkey (93/7)
2	c. finely diced sweet onion
1	c. finely diced celery
2	c. finely shredded cabbage
1½	Tbsp. finely minced fresh ginger
¼	c. finely minced jalapeño, seeds and ribs removed
2	egg whites
½	c. Whole-Wheat Bread Crumbs, *pg. 163*
¼	c. low-sodium soy sauce
2	tsp. toasted sesame oil
2	Tbsp. sweet Asian chili sauce
3	packets stevia or 2 Tbsp. sugar
	salt and pepper to taste

INSTRUCTIONS

1. Preheat oven to 375 degrees.
2. Combine all ingredients and mix thoroughly.
3. Roll mixture into 40 quarter-size meatballs.
4. Put meatballs on a nonstick baking sheet sprayed with nonstick cooking spray.
5. Bake in oven for 25 to 30 minutes, or until meatballs are thoroughly cooked.

"If you're going to make meatballs, make sure it's these! Bring these to your parties or throw in the freezer to eat or add to any dish. These are definitely a crowd pleaser, so don't plan on any leftovers!"

Nutritional Value
Nutritional information based on 1 meatball.

Calories: 38   Fat: 1g   Carbohydrates: 1g   Protein: 4g   Sugar: <1g

pizza tartlets

Makes 15 tartlets.

INGREDIENTS

- ⅓ c. finely diced mushrooms and red bell pepper
- 2 Tbsp. finely diced onion
- 2-3 Tbsp. pizza sauce
- ¼ c. Italian Turkey Sausage, *pg. 121*
- ¼ c. finely diced turkey pepperoni
- ¼ c. shredded, low-fat mozzarella cheese
- 1 box (15 count) mini phyllo cups
- salt and pepper to taste

INSTRUCTIONS

1. Preheat oven to 375 degrees.
2. Put finely diced mushroom, onion and pepper in microwave-safe bowl. Microwave on high for 1 minute.
3. Add remaining ingredients and mix well.
4. Fill mini phyllo cups with mixture.
5. Bake in oven for 12 to 15 minutes.

"Cute, impressive and heavenly. These little mini bites of pizza are always a hit. They pack so much flavor and are just what the doctor ordered when the mood for a big slice arises! Who doesn't like a party where there's pizza?"

Nutritional Value
Nutritional information based on 1 tartlet.

Calories: 29   Fat: 1g   Carbohydrates: 3g   Protein: 2g   Sugar: <1g

stuffed mushrooms

Makes 20 to 24 stuffed mushrooms
(depending on mushroom size).

INGREDIENTS

16	oz. fresh portabella mushrooms (be sure to remove, finely chop and include the mushroom stems, too)
¾	c. Italian Turkey Sausage, *pg. 121*
2	Tbsp. dried bread crumbs
1	packet stevia or 2 tsp. sugar (optional)
½	c. finely chopped onion
½	c. finely chopped celery
1	c. shredded, low-fat mozzarella cheese
2	Tbsp. grated Parmesan
1	egg white
	salt and pepper to taste

INSTRUCTIONS

1. Preheat oven to 375 degrees.

2. Remove stems from mushroom caps and finely chop the stems.

3. Sauté onions, celery and chopped stems until tender. Cool.

4. Combine onion mixture, sausage, cheese, egg white and bread crumbs, and mix well.

5. Stuff the mushrooms with mixture.

6. Bake for about 15 to 20 minutes or until golden.

> *"These are one of my most popular recipes.
> Easy to make, take and pop in your mouth!"*

Nutritional Value
Nutritional information based on 1 stuffed mushroom.

Calories: 29   Fat: 2g   Carbohydrates: 1g   Protein: 4g   Sugar: <1g

salads, dressings
& soups

avocado egg salad

Makes 8 servings.

INGREDIENTS

  1 c. chopped celery

  ¼ c. each finely chopped black olives and green olives

  ¼ c. finely chopped walnuts

10 large hard-boiled eggs (remove and discard 8 of the yolks after cooking)

  2 avocados (chopped and pits removed)

  ½ c. fat-free greek yogurt

  ¼ c. low-fat mayo

  ½ tsp. dijon mustard

     pinch of cayenne pepper

     pinch of dill weed

     lettuce leaves

     salt and pepper to taste

INSTRUCTIONS

1. Dice hard-boiled eggs (2 eggs with yolks and 8 eggs without yolks). Combine eggs, celery, walnuts, olives and avocados in large bowl.

2. In separate bowl combine yogurt, mayo, mustard, cayenne and dill weed and mix well. Add mayo mixture to egg mixture and stir well until fully mixed.

3. Scoop half of egg salad into a lettuce cup of your choice and enjoy!

note:

To keep avocados from turning brown, chop avocado and soak in salt water (1/4 c. sea salt and 2 c. water stirred until salt desolves) for 5 minutes. Remove from water and pat with paper toweling.

Nutritional Value
Nutritional information is based on 1/2 cup.

Calories: 160   Fat: 12g   Sodium: 320mg   Carbohydrates: 6g   Fiber: 3g   Sugar: 1g   Protein: 8g

tomato cucumber salad with feta

Makes 6 servings.

INGREDIENTS

- 1 c. chopped celery
- 2 tomatoes, sliced and halved
- 1 cucumber, thinly sliced
- ½ c. reduced-fat crumbled feta
- 6 basil leaves, chopped
- 2 Tbsp. olive oil
- 2 tsp. honey
- 1 Tbsp. white wine vinegar
  salt and pepper to taste

INSTRUCTIONS

Dressing

1. Mix olive oil, honey, white wine vinegar until mixed well. Set aside.

For the Salad

1. Mix together tomatoes, cucumbers, and basil.
2. Add dressing to the veggies, and stir to coat all the veggies well.
3. Add feta cheese and stir lightly.

Nutritional Value
Nutritional information is based on 1/6 of recipe.

Calories: 80 ❀ Fat: 6g ❀ Sodium: 215mg ❀ Carbohydrates: 6g ❀ Fiber: 1g ❀ Sugar: 4g ❀ Protein: 2g

tuna-mole

Makes 2 servings.

INGREDIENTS

- 1 4 oz. can of tuna in water, drained
- ½ avocado
- ¼ cup chopped red onion
- 4 grape tomatoes, quartered
  lemon juice to taste
  salt to taste

INSTRUCTIONS

1. In a bowl, combine all ingredients and mix well.
2. Serve on a salad or with a slice of bread, rice cake or crackers.

Submitted by Christina Hall of North Carolina

Nutritional Value
Nutritional information is based on 1/2 of recipe.

Calories: 165 ❀ Fat: 8g ❀ Sodium: 440mg ❀ Carbohydrates: 7g ❀ Fiber: 4g ❀ Sugar: 2g ❀ Protein: 18g

yummy chicken salad

Makes about 12 servings.

INGREDIENTS

- 4   4 oz. roasted, boneless skinless chicken breasts
- 1   c. celery, diced
- ½   c. sweet red pepper, diced
- ¼   c. sweet onion, finely diced
- ½   c. black olives, chopped
- ½   c. toasted walnuts, chopped
- ¼   c. dried cranberries
- 1   c. fat-free Greek yogurt
- ¼   c. low-fat mayo
- ½   tsp. dried tarragon
- ½   tsp. dried thyme
- 1-2   packets stevia or natural sweetener of choice
-   salt and pepper to taste

INSTRUCTIONS

1. Preheat oven to 350 degrees.
2. Roast chicken breasts for 25-30 mins, or until chicken juice runs clear.
3. Chop chicken into bite-sized pieces.
4. Add celery, peppers, olives, onions, walnuts and dried cranberries.
5. Mix together yogurt, mayo, tarragon, thyme and stevia.
6. Mix into chicken mixture.
7. Chill for 1-2 hours.

tips:

No time to cook? Just pick up a pre-roasted chicken from your favorite deli, and debone and de-skin the chicken and break into bite-sized pieces. Then follow the recipe.

Can use the frozen pre-chopped onion, celery, and pepper mixture from your grocery freezer section. This makes a wonderful chicken sandwich or is excellent on top of your favorite lettuce.

Nutritional Value
Nutritional information is based on 1/2 cup.

Calories: 115   Fat: 5g   Sodium: 170mg   Carbohydrates: 6g   Fiber: 1g   Sugar: 3g   Protein: 11g

veggie potato salad

Makes 12 servings.

INGREDIENTS

Salad

5	medium red potatoes
5	c. cauliflower florets
⅔	c. radishes, diced
1	c. English cucumber, diced
½	c. red onion, diced
1	c. celery, diced
6	hard-boiled egg whites, diced

Dressing

6	oz. fat-free Greek yogurt
½	c. low-fat mayo
1	Tbsp. dijon mustard
¾	c. low-fat buttermilk
½	tsp. dried tarragon leaves
½	tsp. garlic powder
1	Tbsp. light olive oil
2	packets stevia or 4 tsp. sugar

INSTRUCTIONS

1. Boil potatoes, drain and cool. Dice potatoes into half-inch cubes.

2. Steam cauliflower until tender, dice cauliflower.

3. Mix all salad ingredients together.

4. In separate bowl, combine all dressing ingredients and whisk together until thoroughly mixed.

5. Add dressing to salad ingredients and mix well.

6. Let sit in refrigerator for at least 1 hour before serving.

> *"You never have go to a picnic empty handed when you have this tasty recipe! The best part is knowing you have something healthy to eat while you're there!"*

Nutritional Value
Nutritional information is based on 1 cup of salad.

Calories: 131 ❋ Fat: 2g ❋ Carbohydrates: 19g ❋ Protein: 7g ❋ Sugar: 4g

bean and veggie salad

Makes 6 servings.

INGREDIENTS

¾   c. each canned black beans, chick peas and great northern beans (drained and rinsed)

½   c. diced red onion

1   c. (heaping) diced fresh tomatoes

1   c. each diced English cucumbers, red bell pepper and celery

2-3   oz. crumbled goat cheese

     salt and pepper to taste

     Balsamic Dressing, *pg. 66*

INSTRUCTIONS

1. Combine all ingredients, and mix well.
2. Dress with Balsamic Dressing.

"One of the most amazing things about eating healthy is you actually start craving vegetables! I never thought it would happen to me. This salad is so fresh and satisfying, and the goat cheese is the perfect complement to this dish!"

Nutritional Value
Nutritional information is based on 1 cup of salad. Dressing not included.

Calories: 46   Fat: 2g   Carbohydrates: 3g   Protein: 5g   Sugar: <1g

greek orzo salad

Makes about 4 servings.

INGREDIENTS

⅔ c. whole-wheat orzo, uncooked

2 c. fresh tomatoes, diced

1 c. English cucumber, diced

1 small diced red onion

1 diced green bell pepper

½ c. diced black or kalamata olives

3 oz. crumbled fat-free feta cheese

½ c. Greek Dressing, *pg. 68*

INSTRUCTIONS

1. Cook orzo according to directions on package. Drain and cool.
2. Mix all ingredients together.
3. Add dressing and mix well.

"Even your yia yia would approve of this one! Healthy and mouth watering!"

Nutritional Value

Nutritional information is based on ¼ of salad.

Calories: 202   Fat: 5g   Carbohydrates: 22g   Protein: 10g   Sugar: 4g

salad niçoise

Makes 4 heaping servings.

INGREDIENTS

1	c. blanched green beans
2	medium red potatoes, cooked and chopped
⅓	c. diced red onion
½	c. black or kalamata olives
3	hard-boiled egg whites, chopped
¾	c. diced red bell pepper
1	c. diced fresh tomato
2	5 oz. cans solid white tuna, drained and chopped
4	c. chopped romaine lettuce
	Greek Dressing, *pg. 68*

INSTRUCTIONS

1. Blanch green beans for two minutes in boiling water until bright green.

2. Drain and rinse in cold water to stop cooking process.

3. Cook potatoes and let cool. Chop into half-inch cubes.

4. Combine all salad ingredients and mix well.

5. Add ½ c. Greek Dressing and mix well.

6. Serve immediately.

Nutritional Value
Nutritional information is based on ¼ of salad.

Calories: 215 ❖ Fat: 5g ❖ Carbohydrates: 18g ❖ Protein: 19g ❖ Sugar: 5g

shrimp salad with avocado dressing

Makes about 4 servings.

INGREDIENTS

1 lb. peeled, deveined, cooked shrimp, chopped

⅔ c. sweet red bell pepper, diced

⅔ c. sweet green bell pepper, diced

1 c. celery, diced

¼ c. red onion, finely diced

   salt and pepper to taste

½ c. Avocado Dressing, *pg. 65*

INSTRUCTIONS

1. Combine shrimp and veggies and mix well. Salt and pepper to taste.

2. Stir in dressing.

3. Serve on a bed of chopped lettuce.

Nutritional Value
Nutritional information is based on ¼ of salad.

Calories: 145 ✿ Fat: 2g ✿ Carbohydrates: 5g ✿ Protein: 23g ✿ Sugar: 2g

smoked salmon pasta salad

Makes 6 servings.

INGREDIENTS

6	oz. whole-wheat macaroni
6	oz. smoked salmon, chopped
¼	c. red onion, diced
1	c. red bell pepper, diced
1	c. frozen baby peas, thawed
1	c. English cucumber, diced
1	c. packed fresh baby spinach
	salt and pepper to taste
¾	c. Buttermilk Dill Dressing, *pg. 70*

INSTRUCTIONS

1. Cook macaroni according to directions. Drain and cool.

2. Mix macaroni, salmon and veggies together.

3. Add dressing and mix well.

4. Let marinate in refrigerator for 1 hour before serving.

Nutritional Value
Nutritional information is based on ⅙ of salad.

Calories: 220 ❀ Fat: 6g ❀ Carbohydrates: 22g ❀ Protein: 13g ❀ Sugar: 4g

strawberry feta spinach salad

Makes about 4 servings.

INGREDIENTS

5	c.	packed fresh baby spinach
¾	c.	fresh tomato, diced
⅓	c.	red onion, diced
¾	c.	sliced strawberries
½	c.	mandarin oranges packed in water, drained
1	c.	English cucumber, diced
⅓	c.	sliced water chestnuts
⅓	c.	crumbled fat-free feta cheese
½	c.	Oriental Dressing, *pg. 67*

INSTRUCTIONS

1. Mix all ingredients together.

2. Pour ½ cup dressing over salad and mix well.

3. Serve immediately. Can add grilled chicken to make a main-course salad packed with protein.

Nutritional Value

Nutritional information is based on ¼ of salad.

Calories: 142   Fat: 4g   Carbohydrates: 15g   Protein: 10g   Sugar: 7g

asparagus walnut salad

Makes 4 heaping servings.

INGREDIENTS

2   c. fresh asparagus (chopped to pea size)

½   c. sweet onion, chopped

¾   c. grated Parmesan cheese

½   c. diced turkey bacon (4-5 cooked slices)

½   c. roasted walnuts, chopped

      drizzle of red wine or balsamic vinegar

      drizzle of your favorite olive oil

      salt and pepper to taste

INSTRUCTIONS

1. Cut lower half of asparagus off, and toss or freeze for asparagus soup.

2. Chop upper half of asparagus into pea-sized pieces.

3. Add all other ingredients to chopped asparagus and mix well.

4. Drizzle with your favorite vinegar and olive oil. Salt and pepper to taste.

5. Chill for 1 to 2 hours.

Don't panic about the fat content, it's good fat (omega 3) from the walnuts.

hint:

Can substitute chicken, turkey or crab in place of the bacon. Just put a cup of the asparagus salad on top of your favorite lettuce, and enjoy.

Nutritional Value

Nutritional information is based on ¼ of salad.

Calories: 236   Fat: 16g   Carbohydrates: 8g   Protein: 14g   Sugar: 3g

japanese steak salad with peanut dressing

Makes about 4 servings.

INGREDIENTS

12	oz. beef tenderloin (grilled medium rare, sliced thinly into strips)
1	c. pea pods, blanched
2	small carrots, julienned
1	small red bell pepper, diced
¼	c. red onion, diced
1	c. celery, diced
1	c. fresh baby bella mushrooms, sliced
6	c. romaine lettuce, chopped
½	c. Japanese Peanut Dressing, *pg. 64*

INSTRUCTIONS

1. Mix all ingredients together.

2. Pour ½ cup dressing over salad and mix well.

3. Serve immediately.

Nutritional Value
Nutritional information is based on ¼ of salad.

Calories: 239   Fat: 9g   Carbohydrates: 7g   Protein: 22g   Sugar: 8g

chicken caesar salad

Makes 4 heaping servings.

INGREDIENTS

4	4 oz. grilled boneless, skinless chicken breasts
6	c. romaine lettuce, diced
1	small red onion, sliced very thin
4	hard-boiled egg whites, chopped
1	c. Whole-Wheat Croutons, *pg. 163*
2	Tbsp. grated Parmesan cheese
	salt and pepper to taste
½	c. Caesar Dressing, *pg. 69*

INSTRUCTIONS

1. Slice grilled chicken in thin strips.
2. Mix all other ingredients together.
3. Top with ¼ of chicken strips.
4. Drizzle with Caesar Dressing.

"I am a salad junkie and I know a good Caesar when I see one. I could seriously eat salad every day and be happy! My husband and I like to rate all of our Caesar salads whenever we're traveling. This recipe is still one of the best!"

Nutritional Value
Nutritional information is based on ¼ of salad.

Calories: 244   Fat: 7g   Carbohydrates: 7g   Protein: 34g   Sugar: 3g

asian coleslaw

Makes about 9 cups.

INGREDIENTS

Dressing
- ¼ c. toasted sesame oil
- ¼ c. white wine or rice wine vinegar
- ¼ c. low-sodium chicken broth
- 2 Tbsp. low-sodium soy sauce
- 5 packets stevia or 3 Tbsp. sugar
- ¼–½ tsp. red pepper flakes

Coleslaw
- 2 Tbsp. light butter
- ¼ c. sliced or slivered almonds
- 1 Tbsp. sesame seeds
- 2 oz. Chinese noodles misna
  (in Oriental foods aisle)
- 1 16 oz. bag coleslaw cabbage mix
- 1 c. diced celery
- 1 c. diced snap peas
- ¾ c. diced green onion
- 1 8 oz. can diced water chestnuts

INSTRUCTIONS

Dressing:
1. Combine dressing ingredients in covered jar and shake well.

Coleslaw:
2. Melt butter in skillet. Brown noodles, almonds and sesame seeds. Remove noodle mixture onto a paper towel to cool.
3. Toss cabbage, celery, snap peas, green onion, water chestnuts and noodle mixture in large bowl. Add dressing and toss well. Salt and pepper to taste.
4. Let stand for 20 minutes before serving.

> *"To serve as an entree, add 4 oz. cooked chicken to coleslaw. I love to use chopsticks to savor every little bite!"*

Nutritional Value

Nutritional information is based on 1 cup.

Calories: 140   Fat: 9g   Carbohydrates: 9g   Protein: 3g   Sugar: 2g

japanese peanut dressing

Makes ¾ cup.

INGREDIENTS

2	Tbsp. natural peanut butter or powdered peanut butter
2	Tbsp. lemon juice
2	Tbsp. soy sauce
3	Tbsp. natural maple syrup
1½	tsp. sesame oil
¼	tsp. garlic powder
¼	tsp. ground ginger
¼	c. chicken stock
	salt and pepper to taste

INSTRUCTIONS

1. Mix all ingredients together in blender on medium speed until well blended.

Nutritional Value
Nutritional information is based on 1 Tbsp.

Calories: 24   Fat: 2g   Carbohydrates: 2g   Protein: <1g   Sugar: <1g

avocado dressing

Makes about 1½ cups.

INGREDIENTS

1 avocado
¼ c. low-fat buttermilk
5 oz. fat-free Greek yogurt
¼ c. chicken stock
¼ c. lime juice
1 tsp. chili powder
¼ tsp. each garlic powder and onion powder
1 packet stevia or 2 tsp. sugar

INSTRUCTIONS

1. Remove pit from avocado. Scoop avocado out of shell. Put avocado and remaining ingredients in blender. Blend on high speed until creamy.

2. Store in glass container. Put plastic wrap on top of dressing in container so dressing is not exposed to air. Put cover on container and store in the refrigerator.

** If desired, recipe can easily be divided in half.**

Nutritional Value
Nutritional information is based on 1 Tbsp.

Calories: 15   Fat: 1g   Carbohydrates: 1g   Protein: 1g   Sugar: 1g

balsamic dressing

Makes ½ cup.

INGREDIENTS

2	Tbsp. balsamic vinegar
1½	Tbsp. lemon juice
1	Tbsp. light olive oil
⅓	c. low-sodium chicken stock
¼	tsp. garlic powder
1	packet stevia or 2 tsp. sugar
	salt and pepper to taste

INSTRUCTIONS

1. Mix all ingredients together in blender on low speed until well blended.

Nutritional Value
Nutritional information is based on 1 Tbsp.

Calories: 17   Fat: 2g   Carbohydrates: <1g   Protein: 0g   Sugar: <1g

oriental dressing

Makes ¾ cup.

INGREDIENTS

5	tsp. rice wine vinegar
4	tsp. soy sauce
1	Tbsp. lemon juice
1	tsp. sesame seeds
1	tsp. dijon mustard
1	Tbsp. light olive oil
1½	tsp. sesame oil
¼	c. low-sodium chicken stock
2	packets stevia or 1½ Tbsp. sugar

INSTRUCTIONS

1. Mix all ingredients together in blender on low speed until well blended.

Nutritional Value
Nutritional information is based on 1 Tbsp.

Calories: 19 ⬥ Fat: 2g ⬥ Carbohydrates: <1g ⬥ Protein: <1g ⬥ Sugar: <1g

greek dressing

Makes ¾ cup.

INGREDIENTS

2	Tbsp. lemon juice
2	Tbsp. red wine vinegar
¼	tsp. garlic powder
1	tsp. dried oregano
1½	Tbsp. light olive oil
¼	c. chicken stock
1	packet stevia or 2 tsp. sugar

INSTRUCTIONS

1. Mix all ingredients together in blender on low speed until well blended.

Nutritional Value
Nutritional information is based on 1 Tbsp.

Calories: 17   Fat: 2g   Carbohydrates: <1g   Protein: 0g   Sugar: <1g

caesar salad dressing

Makes ⅔ cup.

INGREDIENTS

1	hard-boiled egg yolk
4	tsp. lemon juice
1	Tbsp. red wine vinegar
¼	tsp. garlic powder
1	Tbsp. light olive oil
1½	tsp. dijon mustard
1	Tbsp. grated Parmesan
¼	c. chicken stock

INSTRUCTIONS

1. Mash egg yolk with a fork.

2. Add yolk and Parmesan to chicken stock and heat on stove, stirring until yolk is dissolved. Cool stock.

3. Mix all ingredients in blender on medium speed until well blended.

4. Salt and pepper to taste.

Nutritional Value
Nutritional information is based on 1 Tbsp.

Calories: 20 ❀ Fat: 2g ❀ Carbohydrates: <1g ❀ Protein: 5g ❀ Sugar: <1g

buttermilk dill dressing

Makes 1 cup.

INGREDIENTS

- ½   c. + 2 Tbsp. low-fat buttermilk
- ¼   c. fat-free Greek yogurt
- 2   Tbsp. low-fat mayo
- 2   Tbsp. lemon juice
- 1   Tbsp. olive oil
- 1½ tsp. dried dill weed
- ¼   tsp. garlic powder
- 1   packet stevia or 2 tsp. sugar

INSTRUCTIONS

1. Thoroughly mix all ingredients. Store in glass container and keep refrigerated.

Nutritional Value
Nutritional information is based on 1 Tbsp.

Calories: 16 ❀   Fat: 1g ❀   Carbohydrates: 1g ❀   Protein: 1g ❀   Sugar: 1g

pumpkin coconut soup

Makes about 10 servings.

INGREDIENTS

1	Tbsp. olive oil
1	small onion, finely chopped
2	medium Golden Delicious apples, peeled, cored, finely chopped
1	12 oz. bag cauliflower
2	Tbsp. whole-wheat flour
1	tsp. cumin
2	Tbsp. curry powder
⅛	tsp. chili powder
3	c. low-sodium chicken broth
2	15 oz. cans pumpkin
½	c. light unsweetened coconut milk
12	oz. unsweetened, no-sugar-added coconut water
	salt and pepper to taste
	plain 0% Greek yogurt, for serving, optional

INSTRUCTIONS

1. Add onion, apples and cauliflower, and sauté until tender and golden – about 8 minutes.

2. Sprinkle flour, cumin, curry and chili powders over onion mixture, and stir for 1 minute (mixture will be dry).

3. Gradually whisk in broth and cook until mixture begins to thicken.

4. Whisk in pumpkin and coconut milk.

5. Season with salt, pepper and sugar.

6. Bring to a low boil and cook for 5 minutes, stirring often.

7. Reduce heat and simmer for 10 minutes.

8. Remove from heat and let cool slightly.

tip:

Add 2 c. cottage cheese if you want to add more protein or creaminess!
If you prefer more sweetness, add 1-2 Tbsp. brown sugar or stevia.

Nutritional Value
Nutritional information is based on 1¼ cup.

Calories: 135 ❄ Fat: 3g ❄ Sodium: 330mg ❄ Carbohydrates: 25g ❄ Fiber: 7g ❄ Sugar: 11g ❄ Protein: 3g

italian wedding soup

Makes 15 servings.

INGREDIENTS

2	tsp. olive oil
1	c. onion, diced
1	c. celery , diced
¾	c. red or green sweet pepper, diced
2	Tbsp. minced garlic
2	Tbsp. light butter (or olive oil)
3	Tbsp. flour
½	c. red wine (or beef stock)
1	15 oz. can diced tomatoes
4	c. chicken stock
4	c. beef stock
2	bay leaves
1½	tsp. Italian seasoning
⅛	tsp. red pepper flakes
4	packets stevia or 3 Tbsp. sugar
1	lb. ground turkey sausage
2	c. cooked whole-grain orzo (1 c. uncooked)
10	oz. frozen chopped spinach, thawed and drained
½	c. low-fat buttermilk
⅓	c. grated Parmesan

"When I was little, I was obsessed with soup. My grandma used to take me out for soup all the time. She still tells me stories about how it was the only thing I ever ordered. This soup is perfect for cold winter nights, but also goes perfect with Lori Harder's Caesar Salad in the summer. And nothing makes me feel better than some hot soup if I am a little under the weather."

INSTRUCTIONS

1. Sauté celery, onion, sweet pepper and garlic in olive oil until tender (4 to 5 minutes).
2. Stir in butter and flour — cook for 1 minute.
3. Add wine and stir until thickened.
4. Add chicken stock, beef stock and diced tomatoes, and bring to a soft boil.
5. Turn heat down to low and add bay leaves, Italian seasoning and red pepper flakes. Add turkey sausage, cooked orzo and spinach. Stir in buttermilk, sweetener and Parmesan.
6. Simmer for 15 to 20 minutes.

hint:

Soup freezes well. Divide into 1-cup containers and freeze. Just grab a container to take with you to work, microwave, and enjoy a great healthy lunch!

Nutritional Value
Nutritional information is based on 1 cup.

Calories: 130 ❋ Fat: 4g ❋ Carbohydrates: 9g ❋ Protein: 10g ❋ Sugar: 2g

sides

homestyle slow-cooked mashed potatoes

Makes 16 servings.

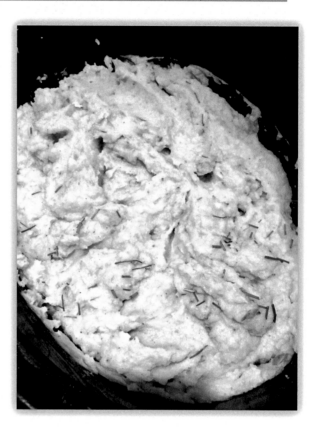

INGREDIENTS

- 3 lbs. golden Yukon potatoes
- 2 lbs. frozen organic cauliflower, thawed
- 3 cloves of peeled garlic
- 4 Tbsp. light butter
- ¼ c. organic low-sodium chicken broth or water
- ¼ c. Greek yogurt
- ½ c. skim milk
- ¼ c. grated Parmesan cheese
- 2 Tbsp. chopped fresh chives – save some for garnish
  salt and pepper to taste

INSTRUCTIONS

1. Put the first five ingredients in a slow cooker and stir together. Place on High for 3-4 hours or on Low for 6-8 hours.

2. When cooking time is complete, add the remaining ingredients into the slow cooker and mash with a hand mixer or immersion blender. Garnish with remaining chives.

Nutritional Value
Nutritional information is based on 3/4 cup.

Calories: 95   Fat: 2g   Sodium: 150mg   Carbohydrates: 17g   Fiber: 2g   Sugar: 3g   Protein: 4g

irish cabbage

Makes about 7 servings.

INGREDIENTS

12	slices turkey bacon
1	medium red onion, diced
1	small/medium head of cabbage, chopped
⅓	c. rice vinegar
1	Tbsp. garlic olive oil
½	tsp. caraway seed
	salt and pepper to taste

INSTRUCTIONS

1. Cut turkey bacon into 1/4- to 1/2-inch strips. Brown bacon in large frying pan with the onion.

2. Add the cabbage and fry for another 10 mins.

3. Add rice vinegar, garlic, olive oil and caraway seeds. Mix and sauté until well blended. Salt and pepper to taste.

4. Can serve warm or at room temperature.

Nutritional Value
Nutritional information is based on 2/3 cup.

Calories: 125　　Fat: 5g　　Sodium: 430mg　　Carbohydrates: 11g　　Fiber: 4g　　Sugar: 6g　　Protein: 13g

maple rainbow carrots

Makes about 7 servings.

INGREDIENTS

2   lbs. rainbow carrots

2   tsp. olive oil

1   tsp. fresh rosemary, finely chopped

1   Tbsp. maple syrup

1   tsp. maple syrup to drizzle on top
    salt and pepper to taste

INSTRUCTIONS

1.   Preheat oven to 425 degrees.

2.   Peel and julienne carrots. Toss with olive oil,
     rosemary and maple syrup.

3.   Bake for 20-25 minutes or until tender.
     Salt and pepper to taste.

4.   Place in serving bowl and drizzle with
     1 tsp. maple syrup.

Nutritional Value
Nutritional information is based on 2/3 cup.

Calories: 70   Fat: 1g   Sodium: 180mg   Carbohydrates: 13g   Fiber: 1g   Sugar: 7g   Protein: 28g

sweet potato and kale casserole

Makes 8 servings.

INGREDIENTS

4-5	medium sweet potatoes
5	oz. container of fresh organic baby kale
½	c. sweet onion, finely diced
2	pears, cored, peeled and sliced
1	c. shredded Parmesan cheese
1	c. fat-free or low-fat plain Greek yogurt
1	c. skim milk (can use unsweetened coconut milk)
¼	tsp. ground cinnamon
¼	tsp. ground nutmeg
	salt and pepper

INSTRUCTIONS

1. Preheat oven to 375 degrees.

2. Use a mandolin to slice the potatoes into
    1/8- to 1/4-inch slices. Spray a 9- by 14-inch
    glass baking dish.

3. Spread half of the sliced sweet potatoes on bottom of dish.
    Layer the top of potatoes with kale. Next top kale with
    1/2 cup Parmesan, onion and pears. Then, put the rest of the
    sweet potatoes on top. Sprinkle with rest of the Parmesan.

4. In a bowl, mix together the milk, yogurt, cinnamon and nutmeg.

5. Carefully pour milk mixture over sweet potato casserole. Salt and pepper to taste.

6. Cover casserole with foil and bake for 20 minutes. Remove foil and
    bake for another 20-25 minutes or until sweet potatoes are thoroughly cooked.

7. Remove from oven and let rest for 10-15 minutes before serving.

Nutritional Value
Nutritional information is based on 3/4 cup.

Calories: 205 ● Fat: 6g ● Sodium: 330mg ● Carbohydrates: 31g ● Fiber: 5g ● Sugar: 12g ● Protein: 12g

roasted bacon asparagus

Makes 10 servings.

INGREDIENTS

- 5 c. fresh asparagus, diced into 1-inch pieces
- 1 c. onions, diced
- 6-8 slices organic turkey bacon, diced
- 8 oz. fresh mushrooms, diced
- ¼ c. chopped walnuts
- 2 Tbsp. organic olive oil

INSTRUCTIONS

1. Preheat oven to 375 degrees. Spray roasting pan with organic olive oil.

2. Mix all ingredients together and spread out on roasting pan.

3. Bake for 20-25 minutes, stirring halfway through baking time.

4. Salt and pepper to taste. Place in serving bowl and enjoy.

Nutritional Value
Nutritional information is based on 1/2 cup.

Calories: 100 ● Fat: 6g ● Sodium: 160mg ● Carbohydrates: 8g ● Fiber: 3g ● Sugar: 3g ● Protein: 8g

broccoli cheddar rice casserole

Makes 12 servings.

INGREDIENTS

2	16 oz. bags frozen broccoli, thawed
16	oz. fresh mushrooms, chopped
1	medium sweet onion, diced
2	Tbsp. flour
2	Tbsp. melted light butter
½	c. fat-free plain Greek yogurt
2	Tbsp. dijon mustard
1	tsp. garlic powder
1½	c. skim milk
1¼	c. shredded sharp cheddar cheese (save ¼ cup for topping)
½	c. grated parmesan cheese
1 c.	uncooked brown rice
1	8 oz. can water chestnuts, drained and chopped

INSTRUCTIONS

1. Preheat oven to 375 degrees.

2. Cook rice according to directions.

3. Wrap thawed broccoli in paper towel to dry.

4. In large mixing bowl, combine mushrooms, onion, broccoli, rice, water chestnuts and flour, and mix well.

5. In another bowl, mix yogurt, milk, mustard, 1 cup cheddar cheese, parmesan cheese, melted butter, garlic powder, and stir well.

6. Pour milk mixture over broccoli mixture, and mix well.

7. Transfer broccoli mixture to a 9 x 13 glass baking dish. Bake for 30-40 minutes until bubbly.

8. Remove from oven and sprinkle top with remaining 1/4 cup cheddar cheese, and bake for an additional 10 minutes or until cheese on top is slightly brown.

9. Remove from oven and let rest for 10 minutes.

Nutritional Value
Nutritional information is based on 2/3 cup.

Calories: 155 ● Fat: 6g ● Sodium: 260mg ● Carbohydrates: 18g ● Fiber: 3g ● Sugar: 3g ● Protein: 11g

roasted butternut rounds with pear sauce

Makes about 10 servings.

INGREDIENTS

- 1-2   butternut squash (with long necks)
- 1   tsp. brown sugar
-     salt and pepper to taste
- 1   c. sweet onion, diced
- 1   Tbsp. light butter
- 2   large pears, peeled and diced
- ½   c. white wine (can use apple juice)
- 1   Tbsp. maple syrup
- ¼   c. chopped pecans
- 2   Tbsp. feta cheese crumbles

INSTRUCTIONS

1. Preheat oven to 400 degrees.

2. Peel necks of squash (save rest of squash for a different recipe). Cut squash into 3/4-inch rounds. Put squash rounds onto baking sheet sprayed with olive oil spray. Sprinkle brown sugar on top of rounds. Salt and pepper to taste. Bake for 25-30 minutes or until tender.

3. Melt butter in sauté pan, add onions and cook until onions are caramelized (about 15-20 minutes).

4. Add wine and maple syrup, and cook for 5 minutes.

5. Add pears and continue to cook until liquid cooks down to half.

6. Spoon mixture onto squash rounds, sprinkle with pecans and feta cheese, and serve.

Nutritional Value
Nutritional information is based on 1 squash round.

Calories: 115   Fat: 3g   Sodium: 85mg   Carbohydrates: 21g   Fiber: 3g   Sugar: 9g   Protein: 2g

roasted apple butternut squash

Makes about 10 servings.

INGREDIENTS

6	c. butternut squash, peeled and diced into ½-inch squares
4	medium apples, cored and diced into ½-inch squares
1½	c. celery, diced
¼	c. + 2 Tbsp. chopped walnuts
¾	c. apple juice
½	tsp. ground cinnamon
¼	tsp. ground nutmeg
	pinch of cayenne pepper
¼	c. kalamata olives, diced
	salt and pepper to taste

INSTRUCTIONS

1. Preheat oven to 375 degrees.

2. In large mixing bowl, combine squash, apples, celery and ¼ c. walnuts.

3. In a glass jar, add apple juice, cinnamon, nutmeg, cayenne pepper, salt and pepper, and shake well.

4. Pour juice mixture over squash mixture and mix well.

5. Transfer to glass baking dish and bake for 30-40 minutes until squash and apples are tender.

6. Remove from oven, stir in olives and top with remaining walnuts.

Nutritional Value
Nutritional information is based on 1 cup.

Calories: 120　●　Fat: 4g　●　Sodium: 180mg　●　Carbohydrates: 22g　●　Fiber: 4g　●　Sugar: 10g　●　Protein: 2g

sweet and smokey onion casserole

Makes 8 servings.

INGREDIENTS

- 5 c. sweet vidalia or walla walla onions, finely diced
- 1½ c. cooked brown rice
- 8 oz. fire-roasted sweet red peppers, drained and finely diced
- ⅓ c. kalamata olives, finely diced
- ½ c. fat-free Greek yogurt
- ½ c. shredded smoked mozzarella cheese
- 2 Tbsp. grated Parmesan cheese
- ⅛ tsp. smokey paprika
- ½ tsp. garlic powder
- 2 tsp. olive oil

INSTRUCTIONS

1. Preheat oven to 325 degrees.

2. Heat 2 tsp. olive oil in a pan over medium heat.
   Add onions and sauté until tender (about 15 minutes).

3. Transfer to large bowl and mix in the remaining ingredients except the Parmesan cheese.

4. Place in an 8- or 9-inch square baking dish, sprinkle the top with the Parmesan cheese.
   Cover with foil and bake for 30 minutes or until bubbly.

Nutritional Value
Nutritional information is based on 1/2 cup.

Calories: 160 ● Fat: 6g ● Sodium: 370mg ● Carbohydrates: 22g ● Fiber: 3g ● Sugar: 6g ● Protein: 6g

brown and wild rice stuffing

Makes 10 servings.

INGREDIENTS

3	c. cooked brown and wild rice mixture
1½	c. celery, diced
8	oz. baby bella mushrooms, diced
1	medium/large sweet onion, diced
1	8 oz. can water chestnuts, diced
1	tsp. fresh sage, finely chopped
½	tsp. fresh rosemary, finely chopped
½	tsp. fresh thyme, finely chopped
½	c. turkey, chicken or vegetable stock
¼	c. low-fat buttermilk

INSTRUCTIONS

1. Preheat oven to 375 degrees.

2. Cook rice according to directions. Sauté mushrooms, celery, onions and water chestnuts until tender and crisp. Mix in herbs, stock and buttermilk.

3. Place in a sprayed 9 x 9 baking dish and bake for 25-30 minutes.

Nutritional Value
Nutritional information is based on 1/2 cup.

Calories: 100 ● Fat: .5g ● Sodium: 80mg ● Carbohydrates: 20g ● Fiber: 3g ● Sugar: 4g ● Protein: 4g

simple roasted vegetables

Makes 5 servings.

INGREDIENTS

5 c. raw vegetables of your choice for roasting (sweet potato, butternut squash, parsnips, Brussels sprouts, cauliflower, broccoli, zucchini, yellow squash, carrots, asparagus, peppers, onion, snap peas etc.)

½ large red onion, chopped

3 garlic cloves, minced

1 tsp. thyme, dried

1 tsp. rosemary, dried

½ tsp. salt and pepper to taste

3 Tbsp. extra-virgin olive oil

Submitted
by
Stacie Hassing
of Minnesota

INSTRUCTIONS

1. Preheat the oven to 375 degrees

2. In a large bowl, combine all of the vegetables and mix them together.

3. Drizzle the olive oil over the vegetables and add the seasonings.

4. Toss to coat.

5. Pour vegetables onto a baking dish, cover with foil and roast in the oven for about 25-30 minutes.

6. Remove foil and bake 5 minutes longer, and serve.

tips:

- *May use 5 cups of whatever vegetables you prefer for roasting – a perfect recipe for using up vegetables!*
- *Use leftovers by adding to scrambled eggs or an omelet.*
- *For balsamic roasted vegetables, add 2 Tbsp. of good-quality balsamic vinegar.*

Nutritional Value

Nutritional information is based on 1/5 of recipe (using sweet potato, zucchini, broccoli and carrots).

Calories: 140 ◉ Fat: 9g ◉ Sodium: 140mg ◉ Carbohydrates: 14g ◉ Fiber: 3g ◉ Sugar: 4g ◉ Protein: 2g

slow-cooked apple cranberry sauce

Makes about 24 servings.

INGREDIENTS

12-15	medium/large organic apples
1	12 oz. bag whole cranberries
6-8	oz. apple juice
1	Tbsp. cinnamon
1	tsp. cocoa powder
¼	tsp. ground cayenne pepper
½	c. coconut sugar

INSTRUCTIONS

1. Quarter and core apples. Do not peel. Place in slow cooker.

2. Add remaining ingredients and stir. Cook in slow cooker for 4 hours on low.

3. When done cooking, mash with a hand masher until smooth or desired consistency.

4. Refrigerate overnight and enjoy.

Nutritional Value
Nutritional information is based on 1/2 cup.

Calories: 75　◉　Fat: 0g　◉　Sodium: 0mg　◉　Carbohydrates: 21g　◉　Fiber: 4g　◉　Sugar: 15g　◉　Protein: 0g

coconut brown rice

Makes about 4 large servings.

INGREDIENTS

2¼	c. unsweetened coconut water
1	c. brown rice or long-grain brown rice
2	scallions, chopped
1	Tbsp. coconut oil
2	cloves garlic, minced or 1 Tbsp. minced garlic
1-2	Tbsp. unsweetened coconut flakes
2	Tbsp. sliced almonds, if desired

INSTRUCTIONS

1. Cook brown rice according to package directions, using coconut water instead of regular water. Once rice is cooked, set aside.

2. In a separate pan on medium heat, add coconut oil, sliced almonds, scallions, coconut flakes and garlic.

3. Sauté for 2 to 3 minutes, then add rice. Cook about 3 to 5 minutes longer, stirring frequently.

tip:

Make it a complete meal by adding a pound of sautéed shrimp or chicken.

Nutritional Value
Nutritional information is based on 1/4 of recipe.

Calories: 180 ● Fat: 7g ● Sodium: 140mg ● Carbohydrates: 29g ● Fiber: 2g ● Sugar: 4g ● Protein: 2g

italian-marinated veggies

Makes 7 servings.

INGREDIENTS

- 1 c. julienne carrots
- 1 c. fresh mushrooms, cut in half
- 1 c. green beans, blanched
- 1 c. broccoli florets
- 1 c. cauliflower florets
- 1 c. radishes (quartered)
- 1 c. celery, cut into two-inch pieces

Marinade:

- ¼ c. balsamic vinegar
- ¼ c. low-sodium chicken stock
- 2 Tbsp. extra-virgin olive oil
- ½ tsp. Italian seasoning
- ¼ tsp. garlic powder
- ¼ tsp. onion powder
- 1 packet stevia or 2 tsp. sugar

INSTRUCTIONS

1. In a glass jar with cover, combine all marinade ingredients. Shake well until all ingredients are combined.

2. Pour marinade over veggies and mix well.

3. Let veggies marinate for at least 1 hour before serving.

> *"By request, these are at every family gathering we have! I always fill up on these first so I don't go overboard on the other goodies!"*

Nutritional Value
Nutritional information is based on 1 cup.

Calories: 68 ❂ Fat: 4g ❂ Carbohydrates: 4g ❂ Protein: 2g ❂ Sugar: 2g

italian green beans

Makes 6 servings.

INGREDIENTS

- 1 lb. fresh green beans,
  washed and stems removed
- 1 small red onion, thinly sliced
- 6 oz. fresh portobello mushrooms, sliced
- 1 15 oz. can petite diced tomatoes
  with basil, drained
- ½ tsp. Italian seasoning
- ¼ tsp. garlic powder
- 2 Tbsp. grated Parmesan cheese
- ½ packet stevia or 1 tsp. sugar
  salt and pepper to taste

INSTRUCTIONS

1. Blanche green beans in salted boiling water for 2 minutes. Drain and rinse in cold ice water until cooled to stop the cooking process.

2. Spray nonstick frying pan with nonstick spray. Sauté mushrooms and onions until caramelized (5 to 8 minutes).

3. Add green beans and sauté until tender crisp.

4. Add tomatoes and seasonings. Cook for another 3 minutes.

5. Remove and place on serving platter and sprinkle with the cheese.

Nutritional Value
Nutritional information is based on ⅙ of platter.

Calories: 66 ✿ Fat: 1g ✿ Carbohydrates: 7g ✿ Protein: 3g ✿ Sugar: 5g

mango coconut quinoa

Makes 6 servings.

INGREDIENTS

- ¾ c. quinoa
- 1½ c. coconut milk
- ¼ tsp. each red pepper flakes, garlic powder and cayenne pepper
- 1 small diced red onion
- 1 c. diced red bell pepper
- 1 c. diced English cucumber
- 1 12 oz. bag frozen mangos, thawed and diced
- 2 Tbsp. unsweetened coconut salt and pepper to taste

INSTRUCTIONS

1. Cook quinoa according to package directions, substituting coconut milk in place of the liquid.
2. Add red pepper flakes, garlic powder and cayenne pepper to quinoa before cooking.
3. Add remaining ingredients with cooked quinoa. Mix well. Salt and pepper to taste.

"Add a cabana and I am in heaven! No matter the weather, this dish makes me feel like I'm on a tropical vacation!"

Nutritional Value
Nutritional information is based on ⅙ of dish.

Calories: 156 ❀ Fat: 2g ❀ Carbohydrates: 26g ❀ Protein: 4g ❀ Sugar: 5g

no-sin green bean casserole

Makes 5 cups.

INGREDIENTS

2	medium onions, thinly sliced
8	oz. sliced mushrooms, fresh or canned
2	tsp. extra-virgin olive oil, divided
2	16 oz. bags whole green beans, thawed and dried
1	8 oz. can water chestnuts, slivered
2	tsp. minced garlic
2	Tbsp. flour
½	c. white wine
½	c. low-fat buttermilk
½	c. slivered toasted almonds
2	Tbsp. Parmesan cheese
	salt and pepper to taste

INSTRUCTIONS

1. Preheat oven to 350 degrees.
2. In a large frying pan, add 1 tsp. extra-virgin olive oil, onions and mushrooms. Cook on medium-high heat until onions are almost caramelized.
3. Add green beans, water chestnuts, garlic, salt and pepper to taste. Stir fry until beans are tender crisp.
4. Add 1 tsp. extra-virgin olive oil, flour and cook for 1 minute.
5. Stir in wine and mix well.
6. Stir in buttermilk and almonds.
7. Transfer to a baking dish and sprinkle with 2 Tbsp. Parmesan cheese.
8. Bake until heated through and cheese is golden brown (about 15 to 20 minutes).

"Just the right blend of wine, Parmesan and creaminess. This recipe makes me think, 'Wow, I'm a good cook!' every time I make this! Ha!"

tip:

This recipe can be doubled or tripled, packaged in desired serving sizes and frozen.

Nutritional Value

Nutritional information is based on ⅔ cup.

Calories: 121 ❁ Fat: 3g ❁ Carbohydrates: 16g ❁ Protein: 4g ❁ Sugar: 4g

baked mac & cheese

Makes 6 servings as an appetizer.
Makes 4 servings as an entree.

INGREDIENTS

2   c. whole-wheat elbow noodles
¼   c. whole-wheat flour
2   Tbsp. sea salt
    (and pepper if desired) to taste
1   c. skim milk
4   oz. low-fat shredded Swiss cheese
4   oz. low-fat shredded cheddar chees
⅛   c. *optional* Whole-Wheat Bread Crumbs,
    pg. 163

INSTRUCTIONS

1. Preheat oven to 375 degrees.
2. Boil noodles on stove top according to package directions.
3. Drain noodles and transfer to casserole dish.
   Slowly add whole-wheat flour and milk while stirring.
   Add salt and cheese. Mix well.
4. Sprinkle top with bread crumbs.
5. Bake in oven until top is lightly brown (about 15 to 20 minutes).

Optional

1. Whole-Wheat Bread Crumbs and 2 Tbsp. Parmesan cheese may be sprinkled on top before baking to add a crispy baked layer over the top.

2. You may add more or less cheese to this recipe depending on what you prefer! It does not affect how it cooks or turns out! Feel free to add some veggies or Italian Turkey Sausage (*pg. 121*) for a complete dinner for the family!

> *"This is a recipe from my dear friend, Kristi Youngdahl. We made this together for an episode of Busy Girl TV. This is 100% kid tested and mother approved! The big kids sure like it, too!"*

Nutritional Value
Nutritional information is based on ⅙ or ¼ serving.

Appetizer
Calories: 193 ❀   Fat: 3g ❀   Carbohydrates: 25g ❀   Protein: 9g ❀   Sugar: 4g

Entree
Calories: 290 ❀   Fat: 4g ❀   Carbohydrates: 38g ❀   Protein: 14g ❀   Sugar: 5g

cheesy mashed potatoes

Makes 8 cups.

INGREDIENTS

6	medium potatoes
6	c. frozen cauliflower
⅓	c. fat-free Greek yogurt
4	wedges Laughing Cow® Light Garlic & Herb Cheese
¼–½	tsp. garlic powder
	splash of skim milk
2	Tbsp. Parmesan cheese
	salt and pepper to taste

INSTRUCTIONS

1. Peel potatoes (can leave skins on if desired), cut in half and boil in salted water until tender.

2. Microwave cauliflower according to package directions until very tender.

3. Drain cooked potatoes, add cauliflower, yogurt, cheese, garlic powder. Beat with mixer until it has a creamy consistency. Add a splash of skim milk if mixture is too thick.

4. Salt and pepper to taste.

Nutritional Value
Nutritional information is based on ½ cup.

Calories: 62 ❂ Fat: <1g ❂ Carbohydrates: 11g ❂ Protein: 3g ❂ Sugar: 2g

butternut squash fries

Makes 2 servings.

INGREDIENTS

1 medium butternut squash
  salt
  chili powder
  cooking spray

INSTRUCTIONS

1. Preheat oven to 425 degrees.
2. Peel squash with potato peeler. Cut into quarters. Scoop out seeds.
3. Use crinkle-cut potato cutter to cut ¼-inch slices.
4. Spray cookie sheet with cooking spray and layer fries in single layer.
5. Sprinkle with salt and chili powder to taste.
6. Bake in oven for 30 to 40 minutes until crisp. Flip fries half way through baking.

"Not to be confused with 'Better-Not' Squash Fries! Now you can indulge, sans the greasy fingers and fat! This is a great side to any lunch or dinner."

Nutritional Value
Nutritional information is based on ½ of the fries.

Calories: 100 ❁ Fat: 0g ❁ Carbohydrates: 20g ❁ Protein: 3g ❁ Sugar: 5g

butternut squash soufflé

Makes 6 cups.

INGREDIENTS

- 4 c. cubed butternut squash, peeled
- ¼–⅓ c. natural maple syrup
- 3 egg whites
- ⅛–¼ tsp. cayenne pepper
- pinch of cinnamon
- ¼ c. pecan pieces
- salt and pepper

INSTRUCTIONS

1. Preheat oven to 350 degrees.
2. Peel and cube butternut squash. Cook in microwave on high for 6 to 8 minutes or until squash is tender.
3. Add remaining ingredients, except egg whites, and beat with mixer until creamy.
4. In separate bowl, beat egg whites until soft peaks form. Gently fold egg whites into squash mixture, ⅓ of egg white mixture at a time. Salt and pepper to taste.
5. Transfer to baking dish and bake for 20-25 minutes.

Nutritional Value
Nutritional information is based on ½ cup.

Calories: 45 ❀ Fat: 2g ❀ Carbohydrates: 5g ❀ Protein: 2g ❀ Sugar: 1g

sweet potato soufflé

Makes 5 cups.

INGREDIENTS

6	large sweet potatoes
1½	c. low-fat buttermilk
¼	c. honey
4	Tbsp. light butter
5	egg whites
½	tsp. cinnamon
10	packets stevia or ⅓ c. sugar
¼	tsp. nutmeg
½	tsp. chili powder
¼	tsp. crushed red pepper flakes
¼	c. chopped pecans
¼	c. natural maple syrup (optional)

INSTRUCTIONS

1. Preheat oven to 350 degrees.
2. Cook sweet potatoes in microwave until soft (about 15 minutes).
3. Slice sweet potatoes in half lengthwise, scoop potato out of skins and into a cooking pot. Heat on medium heat.
4. Add buttermilk, honey, butter, cinnamon, nutmeg, chili powder, red pepper flakes and maple syrup (optional).
5. Mash warm potato mixture or beat with hand mixer for creamier consistency.
6. In separate bowl, beat egg whites with mixer until soft peaks form and gently fold into potato mixture.
7. Transfer to casserole dish, sprinkle with chopped pecans and bake for 20 to 25 minutes or until egg whites are set.

"So light, yet so full of flavor! I love that I don't feel weighed down after eating this. Thanksgiving would not be the same without this side. This could almost pass as a dessert with a few marshmallows thrown on top."

hint:

Don't be concerned about the sugar! The majority of the sugar count comes from the sweet potatoes which naturally have healthy sugars your body uses for energy.

Nutritional Value
Nutritional information is based on ½ cup.

Calories: 152   Fat: 5g   Carbohydrates: 27g   Protein: 6g   Sugar: 11g

entrees

cranberry chicken

Makes 6 servings.

INGREDIENTS

- 6   5 oz. raw chicken breasts
- ½   c. buttermilk
- ¼   c. fat-free or low-fat plain Greek yogurt
- ¼   tsp. garlic powder
- ⅓   c. light dried cranberries
- 2   c. sage and onion bread croutons
- ⅓   c. walnuts
-      salt and pepper to taste

INSTRUCTIONS

1. Preheat oven to 375 degrees.

2. Mix buttermilk, yogurt, garlic powder,
    salt and pepper together. Add chicken breasts
    and marinate for at least 1 hour or overnight.

3. Put cranberries in food processor and pulse until finely chopped.
    Add croutons, walnuts, salt and pepper, and pulse together until finely chopped.

4. Remove crouton mixture and put in bowl. Remove chicken from buttermilk marinade
    and dredge through crouton mixture until chicken is completely covered.

5. Put chicken on baking sheet and cook for 30-40 minutes or until completely cooked.
    Let chicken set for 10 minutes and serve.

> *This dish tastes like Thanksgiving chicken
> and dressing without the dressing — YUM!*

Nutritional Value
Nutritional information is based on 1 chicken breast or 1/6 of recipe.

Calories: 290   Fat: 8g   Sodium: 260mg   Carbohydrates: 16g   Fiber: 1g   Sugar: 8g   Protein: 37g

green curry lettuce cups

Makes 2 servings.

INGREDIENTS

2	4-6 oz. chicken breasts, diced small
1	can chopped water chestnuts
2	Tbsp. green curry paste
⅓	c. organic canned coconut milk
3	green onions, chopped
1	tsp. ground ginger
1	tsp. garlic powder
1	c. finely shredded cabbage
1	small head of bibb lettuce
1	lime, cut into 6 slices
	salt to taste

INSTRUCTIONS

1. In a large frying pan, add everything except cabbage and bibb lettuce.

2. Cook on medium heat for about 15 minutes or until chicken is done.

3. Add cabbage, and cook for about 3-5 minutes more.

4. Wash and separate bibb lettuce.

5. Add about 1/2 cup of chicken mixture into each lettuce cup, squeeze lime on top. Enjoy!

Nutritional Value
Nutritional information is based on 5 lettuce wraps.

Calories: 350 ● Fat: 10g ● Sodium: 430mg ● Carbohydrates: 25g ● Fiber: 3g ● Sugar: 5g ● Protein: 36g

chicken wellington roll

Makes 4 servings.

INGREDIENTS

- 4   sheets phyllo dough
- 4   4 oz. uncooked, boneless skinless chicken breasts
- ¾   c. mushrooms, finely diced
- ¼   c. water chestnuts, finely diced
- ½   c. red onion, finely diced
- ½   tsp. garlic powder
- 3   oz. fat-free cream cheese
- 2   Tbsp. fat-free Greek yogurt
  salt and pepper to taste
  garlic salt
  butter-flavored cooking spray

INSTRUCTIONS

1. Preheat oven to 375 degrees.

2. Sauté mushrooms, onions, water chestnuts and garlic powder in nonstick cooking pan until onions are caramelized.

3. Add cheese and yogurt. Cook until cheese is melted and mixed well. Salt and pepper to taste.

4. Pound each chicken breast to ¼-inch in thickness. Spread ¼ of mushroom mixture on chicken and roll up breast.

5. Roll out 4 sheets of phyllo dough and quarter them with a pizza cutter. Spray 2 of the quartered sheets with cooking spray. Put 2 more quartered sheets on top of sprayed sheets and spray with cooking spray.

6. Place 1 rolled chicken on sprayed sheets and roll up. Spray top of roll with cooking spray and sprinkle with garlic salt.

7. Place seam-side down on a cookie sheet coated with cooking spray. Bake for 20 minutes or until dough is lightly brown and crisp and chicken is not pink inside.

"I love this healthy spin on an old favorite. Talk about an easy way to impress! Anything wrapped in phyllo dough gets an A+ in my book."

Nutritional Value
Nutritional information is based on 1 roll.

Calories: 215   Fat: 3g   Carbohydrates: 11g   Protein: 31g   Sugar: 3g

chicken mushroom quesadilla

Makes 2 servings.

INGREDIENTS

4	oz. grilled chicken breast, cut into thin strips
4	oz. fresh baby bella mushrooms, sliced
1	medium sweet onion, sliced
½	c. shredded low-fat mozzarella cheese
¼	tsp. garlic salt, divided
2	Tbsp. salsa verde
2	large whole-wheat, low-carb tortilla

INSTRUCTIONS

1. Sauté all ingredients, except tortillas and cheese, in a hot nonstick pan coated with cooking spray until chicken and veggies are tender. Salt and pepper to taste.

2. Put half of chicken mixture on half of each tortilla. Cover each chicken mixture with half of cheese.

3. Fold each tortilla over and cook in nonstick pan coated with cooking spray until bottom of tortillas are lightly brown and crisp.

4. Spray top of tortillas with cooking spray and flip them over in the pan. Cook for 2 to 4 minutes or until lightly brown and crisp.

> *"Because we all get the craving at one point or another, be sure to keep the ingredients for this game-day favorite on hand just in 'queso!'... You know you were thinking it!"*

Nutritional Value
Nutritional information is based on 1 quesadilla.

Calories: 279　Fat: 10g　Carbohydrates: 14g　Protein: 30g　Sugar: 4g

greek-marinated chicken breast

Makes 4 servings.

INGREDIENTS

4	4 oz. chicken breasts
1	Tbsp. olive oil
¼	c. balsamic vinegar
1	Tbsp. lemon juice
2	tsp. minced garlic
2	Tbsp. finely diced kalamata olives
2	packets stevia or 1 Tbsp. sugar
¼	tsp. dried oregano
1	tsp. salt

INSTRUCTIONS

1. Put all ingredients into a large plastic bag. Shake/mix ingredients and refrigerate for 1 to 24 hours — the longer the better.

2. Preheat oven to 375 degrees.

3. Remove chicken from bag and put in a baking dish sprayed with nonstick cooking spray.

4. Bake for 25 to 30 minutes or until juice runs clear when chicken is poked with a fork.

"This dish is great served with your favorite salad or with whole-grain orzo and fresh tomato."

Nutritional Value
Nutritional information is based on 1 chicken breast.

Calories: 172   Fat: 7g   Carbohydrates: 2g   Protein: 25g   Sugar: 2g

chicken enchiladas

Makes 6 servings.

INGREDIENTS

- 1   c. salsa verde
- ⅔   c. low-fat buttermilk
- 1   Tbsp. corn starch
- 2   wedges Laughing Cow® Queso Fresco Cheese
- 2   c. cooked chicken breast, shredded
- 1   c. diced red or sweet onion
- 1   c. fat-free cottage cheese
- 2   oz. low-fat monterey cheese, shredded
- 6   large whole-wheat, low-carb tortilla wraps
- 1   packet stevia or 2 tsp. sugar
-     salt and pepper to taste

INSTRUCTIONS

1. Preheat oven to 375 degrees.

2. Sauté onions in nonstick pan until tender. Add cottage cheese, monterey cheese and chicken. Cook until cheese melts and chicken is well blended. Salt and pepper to taste.

3. In separate pan, heat salsa, buttermilk, corn starch, sweetener and Laughing Cow cheese until cheese is melted. Salt and pepper to taste.

4. Fill tortilla with ⅙ of chicken mixture, spread 1 Tbsp. of salsa on chicken and roll tortilla. Repeat with other 5 tortillas. Put in a baking dish sprayed with cooking spray. Cover tortillas with remaining salsa.

5. Bake in oven for 20 to 25 minutes until bubbly and cheese is melted.

> "I love these and still can't believe I get to eat them! This is pretty much where all of my favorite things come together — cheese, tortillas and gooey goodness!"

Nutritional Value
Nutritional information is based on 1 enchilada.

Calories: 254   Fat: 7g   Carbohydrates: 15g   Protein: 25g   Sugar: 4g

asian-marinated chicken breast

Makes 4 servings.

INGREDIENTS

4 4 oz. chicken breasts

1 Tbsp. toasted sesame oil

¼ c. rice wine vinegar

2 Tbsp. low-sodium soy sauce

2 tsp. minced garlic

¼ tsp. ground ginger

2 packets stevia or 1 Tbsp. sugar

¼ tsp. salt

INSTRUCTIONS

1. Put all ingredients into a large plastic bag. Shake/mix ingredients and refrigerate for 1 to 24 hours — the longer the better.

2. Preheat oven to 375 degrees.

3. Remove chicken from bag and put in a baking dish sprayed with nonstick cooking spray.

4. Bake for 25 to 30 minutes or until juice runs clear when chicken is poked with a fork.

5. Great served with your favorite coleslaw, brown rice and pea pods.

Nutritional Value
Nutritional information is based on 1 chicken breast.

Calories: 167 ❀   Fat: 7g ❀   Carbohydrates: 0g ❀   Protein: 25g ❀   Sugar: 0g

chicken & mushroom yogurt sauce

Makes 4 servings.

INGREDIENTS

- 4 4 oz. boneless chicken breasts
- 1 c. diced red onion
- 1 Tbsp. minced garlic
- 2 6 oz. cans sliced mushrooms, drained
- ⅔ c. low-sodium, all-natural chicken stock
- 1 6 oz. container fat-free Greek yogurt
- 3 Tbsp. whole-wheat flour, divided
- 1 tsp. Worcestershire sauce
- 1 packet stevia or 2 tsp. sugar

INSTRUCTIONS

1. Put chicken, 2 Tbsp. flour, salt and pepper in plastic bag. Shake until chicken is coated.

2. Brown chicken in a nonstick pan coated with nonstick cooking spray — about 3 minutes per side.

3. Remove chicken and re-spray pan. Sauté onions, mushrooms and garlic until tender.

4. Return chicken to pan, add broth, cover and simmer chicken 20 to 25 minutes or until chicken is no longer pink, and juices run clear when pierced. Remove and place chicken on serving platter and keep warm.

5. Mix 1 Tbsp. flour and Worcestershire sauce with yogurt until well blended.

6. Add yogurt to pan, mix well and simmer until thickened.

7. Pour sauce over chicken. Serve with brown rice or quinoa.

Nutritional Value
Nutritional information is based on 1 chicken breast.

Calories: 222　　Fat: 3g　　Carbohydrates: 10g　　Protein: 32g　　Sugar: 3g

chicken fingers

Makes 4 servings.

INGREDIENTS

- 1 lb. boneless skinless chicken breast
- ¼ c. fat-free Greek yogurt
- ¼ c. fat-free sour cream
- ¼ c. low-fat buttermilk
- 1 tsp. lemon juice
- 2 tsp. garlic powder, divided
- 1 tsp. onion powder, divided
- ½ tsp. poultry seasoning
- ½ tsp. salt
- ½ c. Whole-Wheat Bread Crumbs, *pg. 163*
- ¼ c. whole-grain cornmeal

INSTRUCTIONS

1. Preheat oven to 400 degrees.
2. Cut chicken breasts into 1-by-3-inch strips.
3. Mix yogurt, sour cream, buttermilk, lemon juice, 1 tsp. garlic powder, ½ tsp. onion powder and poultry seasoning together, and mix with chicken strips.
4. Mix bread crumbs, cornmeal, 1 tsp. garlic powder and ½ tsp. onion powder together.
5. Coat chicken breast strips in bread crumb mixture and put on baking sheet sprayed with cooking spray.
6. Spray chicken strips with cooking spray and bake for 20 minutes.

"Do we ever really outgrow this kid favorite? It feels so good to know you can feed your family something they love while you keep it healthy! Why fry your food when you can make it taste even better without all the fat?"

Nutritional Value
Nutritional information is based on 4 chicken strips.

Calories: 218 ❖   Fat: 3g ❖   Carbohydrates: 11g ❖   Protein: 31g ❖   Sugar: 3g

italian-marinated chicken breast

Makes 4 servings.

INGREDIENTS

- 4   4 oz. boneless chicken breasts
- 1   Tbsp. olive oil
- ¼   c. red wine vinegar
- 1   tsp. Italian seasoning
- 2   tsp. minced garlic
- ¼   tsp. crushed red pepper
- 2   packets stevia or 1 Tbsp. sugar
- 1   tsp. salt

INSTRUCTIONS

1. Put all ingredients into a large plastic bag. Shake/mix ingredients and refrigerate for 1 to 24 hours — the longer the better.

2. Preheat oven to 375 degrees.

3. Remove chicken from bag and put in a baking dish sprayed with nonstick cooking spray.

4. Bake for 25 to 30 minutes or until juice runs clear when chicken is poked with a fork.

"This chicken is great served on top of your favorite salad or with a side of whole-grain rice and grilled veggies."

Nutritional Value
Nutritional information is based on 1 chicken breast.

Calories: 167   Fat: 7g   Carbohydrates: 0g   Protein: 25g   Sugar: 0g

peachy cream chicken

Makes 4 servings.

INGREDIENTS

4	4 oz. boneless skinless chicken breasts
2	Tbsp. whole-wheat flour
1	tsp. olive oil
1	12 oz. bag frozen, sliced peaches, thawed
1	small red onion, thinly sliced
½	c. green pepper, diced
¾	c. low-sodium chicken broth
¼	c. fat-free Greek yogurt
½	tsp. grated lemon peel
2	packets stevia or 1 Tbsp. sugar
6	large basil leaves, rolled up and thinly sliced
¼	tsp. cayenne pepper
	salt and pepper to taste

INSTRUCTIONS

1. Sprinkle chicken breast with flour. Salt and pepper breasts to taste.

2. Add olive oil to nonstick skillet. Add chicken to skillet and cook on medium heat, turning once until chicken is cooked thoroughly (about 15 minutes). Transfer cooked chicken to serving platter and keep warm.

3. Add remaining ingredients (except for sliced basil, lemon peel and yogurt) to skillet and bring to boil.

4. Turn down heat and simmer. Stir frequently until sauce has thickened (about 3 to 5 minutes).

5. Remove sauce from heat and stir in yogurt, lemon and basil. Salt and pepper to taste.

6. Spoon over chicken and serve immediately.

Great served over quinoa or brown rice.

Nutritional Value

Nutritional information is based on 1 chicken breast and ¼ of sauce.

Calories: 210 ❁ Fat: 5g ❁ Carbohydrates: 10g ❁ Protein: 28g ❁ Sugar: 5g

tandoori chicken

Makes 4 servings.

INGREDIENTS

4	4 oz. boneless, skinless chicken breasts
2	limes
1	6 oz. container fat-free Greek yogurt
2	Tbsp. low-fat mayo
½	tsp. each ground ginger, garlic powder and onion powder
1	tsp. each ground coriander and ground cumin
1	Tbsp. smokey paprika
¼	tsp. cayenne pepper
	salt and pepper to taste

INSTRUCTIONS

1. Mix yogurt, mayo, juice of 2 limes and all the spices in a large plastic bag. Add chicken and marinate for 1 hour to 24 hours — the longer the better.

2. Preheat oven to 425 degrees.

3. Put chicken and marinade in roasting pan and bake for 30 minutes or until juices run clear when thickest part of breast is pierced with a fork.

Nutritional Value

Nutritional information is based on 1 chicken breast.

Calories: 167   Fat: 4g   Carbohydrates: 5g   Protein: 29g   Sugar: 3g

chicken pizzaioli

Makes 4 servings.

INGREDIENTS

4	4 oz. boneless, skinless chicken breasts
1	small red onion, diced
1	28 oz. can crushed tomatoes
1½	tsp. dried Italian seasoning
1	tsp. garlic salt
½-1	1 tsp. red pepper flakes
1	tsp. fennel seed
2	Tbsp. chopped fresh basil
2	packets stevia or 2 Tbsp. sugar
¾	c. grated low-fat mozzarella cheese
	salt and pepper to taste

INSTRUCTIONS

1. Preheat oven to 375 degrees.

2. Pound chicken into ½-inch cutlets. Season both sides of cutlets with salt and pepper.

3. Spray oven-safe skillet with cooking spray. Put cutlets in hot skillet and cook for 2 minutes until browned. Flip chicken and brown other side for 2 minutes. Remove chicken.

4. In same pan, sauté onions until soft. Add remaining ingredients (except for cheese and basil) and simmer for 3 minutes. Remove from heat and stir in basil.

5. Transfer chicken to top of tomato mixture. Sprinkle top of cutlets with cheese and bake for 15 to 20 minutes until chicken is thoroughly cooked and cheese is melted.

Goes great with crusty whole-grain Artisan bread and a light salad.

"I love Italian food so this meal makes my belly very happy! If I have to have a little whole-wheat pasta this is a great topper for that. I fill up on the veggies and chicken and keep my starchy side smaller."

Nutritional Value

Nutritional information is based on 1 chicken breast and ¼ of sauce.

Calories: 257   Fat: 6g   Carbohydrates: 10g   Protein: 33g   Sugar: 7g

maple pecan chicken

Makes 4 servings.

INGREDIENTS

- 4 4 oz. boneless, skinless chicken breasts
- 2 Tbsp. natural maple syrup
- ¼ c. pecans
- ¾ c. Whole-Wheat Bread Crumbs, *pg. 163*
- ¼ tsp. cayenne pepper

   salt and pepper to taste

INSTRUCTIONS

1. Preheat oven to 400 degrees.

2. Pound chicken breasts to ¼-inch thickness.

3. Brush chicken with maple syrup.

4. Finely grind pecans in food processor or blender.

5. In a plastic bag, mix pecans, bread crumbs, cayenne pepper and salt. Add chicken to bread mixture and shake to completely cover chicken.

6. Put chicken on baking sheet sprayed with nonstick cooking spray. Spray top of chicken with cooking spray.

7. Bake in oven for 20 to 25 minutes or until chicken is thoroughly cooked.

"Chicken is a staple in so many households, and I believe in keeping it interesting at all times! Nothing like maple and pecans to make this dish irresistible."

Nutritional Value
Nutritional information is based on 1 chicken breast.

Calories: 210   ✿   Fat: 8g   ✿   Carbohydrates: 5g   ✿   Protein: 27g   ✿   Sugar: <1g

mediterranean chicken

Makes 4 servings.

INGREDIENTS

8	small boneless, skinless chicken thighs
2	Tbsp. whole-wheat flour
1	small diced red onion
¼	c. kalamata olives, coarsely chopped
1	15 oz. can petite diced tomatoes
½	c. low-sodium chicken broth
½	tsp. dried oregano
½	tsp. dried basil
½	tsp. garlic powder
1	packet stevia or 2 tsp. sugar
1½	Tbsp. balsamic vinegar
	salt and pepper to taste

INSTRUCTIONS

1. Sprinkle chicken thighs with flour.
2. Put chicken in a large nonstick skillet sprayed with cooking spray.
3. Brown chicken on both sides, remove from skillet.
4. Add onion to skillet and cook until caramelized.
5. Add tomatoes, olives, chicken broth, vinegar and spices. Stir well.
6. Return chicken to skillet and cook on high until boiling.
7. Reduce heat to low, cover and simmer for 25 to 30 minutes or until chicken is cooked thoroughly (occasionally spooning olive mixture over chicken).

Great served over quinoa or brown rice.

"Never eat bland chicken again! My mouth is watering just thinking about how savory this recipe is. Serve this over your favorite grain or on a bed of greens. Try a side of the Greek Dressing (pg. 68) to really wow your taste buds!"

Nutritional Value
Nutritional information is based on 1 chicken breast and ¼ of olive mixture.

Calories: 221 ❖ Fat: 9g ❖ Carbohydrates: 9g ❖ Protein: 23g ❖ Sugar: 4g

santa fe wrap

Makes 7 servings.

INGREDIENTS

- 1 lb. diced, cooked chicken breast
- 1 15 oz. can black beans, drained and rinsed
- 1 c. red bell pepper, diced
- ½ c. sweet onion, diced
- 1 c. corn
- 1 10 oz. can diced tomato with green chilies, drained
- 6 oz. fat-free Greek yogurt
- ⅔ c. salsa verde
-   juice of 1 lime
- 4 packets stevia or 3 Tbsp. sugar
-   salt and pepper to taste
- 7 large whole-wheat tortilla wraps or Joseph's® Lavash Bread

INSTRUCTIONS

1. Combine all ingredients in a large bowl and mix well until all ingredients are blended.

2. Put 1 c. of chicken salad in a tortilla wrap, and enjoy!

> "For an extra special treat, spread 1 slice of ripe avocado on the wrap and then add the Santa Fe salad. You also can try serving on a bed of romaine or shredded lettuce if you don't want to have the wrap."

Nutritional Value
Nutritional information is based on 1 cup of salad and 1 large tortilla wrap.

Calories: 270   Fat: 5g   Carbohydrates: 20g   Protein: 29g   Sugar: 6g

turkey-cran tenderloins

Makes 6 servings.

INGREDIENTS

- 3   8-10 oz. turkey tenderloins
- ¼   c. apple juice
- ½   c. cranberry sauce
- 1   Tbsp. soy sauce
- ¼   tsp. ground ginger
- 1   Tbsp. dijon mustard
- 2   Tbsp. light butter

INSTRUCTIONS

1. Preheat oven to 375 degrees.

2. In mixing bowl combine all ingredients except turkey tenderloins. Mix well.

3. Put tenderloins in large plastic bag and pour cranberry mixture over tenderloins. Mix well until tenderloins are thoroughly covered. Marinate in refrigerator for at least 1 hour.

4. Transfer turkey into a glass baking dish and pour marinade over turkey. Bake uncovered for 35-40 minutes or until tenderloins are cooked through.

5. Put tenderloins on serving dish and cover with aluminum foil to keep warm.

6. Pour cranberry mixture into a sauté pan, bring to a boil and simmer until thickened (about 10 minutes).

7. Slice tenderloins, pour cranberry mixture over and serve.

Nutritional Value
Nutritional information is based on 1 tenderloin or 1/6 of recipe.

Calories: 215   Fat: 6g   Sodium: 250mg   Carbohydrates: 10g   Fiber: 0g   Sugar: 8g   Protein: 30g

turkey tenderloins with sausage dressing

Makes 6 servings.

INGREDIENTS

- 8 oz. baby belle mushrooms, diced
- 1 c. celery, diced
- 1 8 oz. can water chestnuts, diced
- 2 medium apples, diced
- 1 c. Italian Turkey Sausage, *pg. 121*
  (or sausage of choice)
- 2 tsp. fresh sage, finely chopped
- ½ tsp. fresh rosemary, finely chopped
- ¼ c. Whole-Wheat Bread Crumbs, *pg. 163*
- ½ c. low-fat buttermilk
- ½ c. turkey, chicken or vegetable stock
- 3 8-10 oz. turkey tenderloins

  salt and pepper to taste

INSTRUCTIONS

1. Preheat oven to 375 degrees.

2. In a pan, sauté mushrooms, celery, water chestnuts and
   apples until tender crisp. Add herbs, sausage, bread crumbs,
   buttermilk and stock. Mix together and simmer for 2-3 minutes.

3. Transfer to a sprayed 9 x 9 baking dish.

4. Salt and pepper turkey tenderloins and place on top of dressing.

5. Bake for 35-40 minutes or until the tenderloins are cooked.

Nutritional Value
Nutritional information is based on 1/2 tenderloin or 1/6 of the dressing.

Calories: 265 ❀ Fat: 5g ❀ Sodium: 350mg ❀ Carbohydrates: 15g ❀ Fiber: 2g ❀ Sugar: 8g ❀ Protein: 39g

guilt-free thanksgiving

Makes 3 servings.

INGREDIENTS

1 package low-sodium deli turkey, chopped

3 large celery stalks, chopped

½ c. chopped frozen cranberries
(thaw briefly in water so they're still cold
and crunchy when you chop)

½ c. chopped walnuts

½ c. mashed sweet potatoes

cinnamon to taste

stevia to taste

salt and pepper to taste

INSTRUCTIONS

1. Chop turkey, celery, walnuts and cranberries, and mix together in a bowl.

2. Peel and boil one large sweet potato.

3. In a separate bowl, mash and season with cinnamon and stevia to your liking.

4. Spoon 1/3 of the mashed sweet potatoes on a plate and top with 1/3 of the turkey mixture.

Submitted
by
Sheira MacKenzie
of Rhode Island

Nutritional Value
Nutritional information is based on 1/3 of recipe.

Calories: 255 ❀ Fat: 14g ❀ Sodium: 420mg ❀ Carbohydrates: 13g ❀ Fiber: 4g ❀ Sugar: 5g ❀ Protein: 21g

mexican cabbage rolls

Makes 10 cabbage rolls.

INGREDIENTS

10 savoy cabbage leaves
 1 lb. lean ground turkey
 1 c. diced onion
 1 c. diced bell peppers
 1 c. black beans
 2 Tbsp. extra-virgin olive oil
 1 Tbsp. chili powder
 1 Tbsp. garlic powder
 1 Tbsp. onion powder
 ½ tsp. cayenne pepper
 1 lime, juiced
    pinch of salt and pepper
 3 cloves of garlic
    other veggie toppings if desired

Submitted by Sarah Smith of Alberta, Canada

INSTRUCTIONS

1. Pan-cook ground turkey. Add chili powder, onion powder, garlic powder and cayenne pepper. Lastly, add a pinch of salt and pepper.

2. Dice up an onion (I used yellow) and two bell peppers of your choice.

3. Crush garlic and add black beans, the juice of one lime, olive oil and a pinch of salt and pepper to taste. Mix all together in a bowl.

4. Remove the leaves from the savoy cabbage, and gently arrange in a bowl-like formation.

5. Place ground turkey at the bottom of the cabbage bowl and pour the mixture of toppings over the top.

6. Roll the cabbage up like a burrito and eat! Use toothpicks to hold them together if needed.

Nutritional Value
Nutritional information is based on 1 cabbage roll.

Calories: 140   Fat: 7g   Sodium: 180mg   Carbohydrates: 10g   Fiber: 3g   Sugar: 3g   Protein: 12g

stuffed cran-apple turkey roll

Makes 16 to 20 servings.

INGREDIENTS

1	c. celery, diced
1	c. onion, diced
1	8 oz. can water chestnuts, drained and diced
2	5 oz. cans mushrooms, drained and diced
1½	c. herb stuffing croutons
1½-2	c. low-sodium chicken stock
2	medium crisp apples, cored and diced
¼	c. dried cranberries
¼	c. diced walnuts
2	Tbsp. light butter
2	1½ lbs. boneless skinless turkey breasts

INSTRUCTIONS

1. Preheat oven to 375 degrees.

2. Mix celery, onion, water chestnuts, mushrooms, stuffing croutons, apples, cranberries and walnuts together in large mixing bowl.

3. Warm chicken stock and butter in microwave until butter melts.

4. Add chicken stock to crouton mixture and mix thoroughly. Salt and pepper to taste. Let set until croutons are soft and cooled.

5. Pound both turkey breasts to ¼-inch thickness.

6. Put 2 cups stuffing on each turkey breast and roll tightly. Tie each breast with kitchen string (about 6 strings per breast). Spray top of turkey breast with cooking spray.

7. Put turkey breasts in roasting pan and roast in oven for 30 to 35 minutes or until turkey is thoroughly cooked.

8. Let breasts set for a few minutes. Remove string from breasts. Slice each breast into 8 to 10 slices.

Nutritional Value
Nutritional information is based on 1/16 of recipe.

Calories: 141 　　Fat: 3g 　　Carbohydrates: 9g 　　Protein: 17g 　　Sugar: 5g

sloppy turkey joes

Makes 7 cups (21 servings).

INGREDIENTS

2½ lbs. ground turkey (93/7)

1   c. each finely diced red onion, bell pepper, celery, carrots and mushrooms

1   29 oz. can all-natural tomato sauce

½   tsp. each garlic powder and onion powder

1   tsp. Mrs. Dash® All-Natural Table Blend Seasoning

1   tsp. liquid smoke

2   tsp. Worcestershire sauce

2   packets stevia or 1 Tbsp. sugar

    salt and pepper to taste

INSTRUCTIONS

1. Brown ground turkey and all the diced vegetables in large nonstick frying pan until turkey is thoroughly cooked and there is no pink left. Salt and pepper to taste.

2. Add the rest of the ingredients and simmer for 20 minutes.

3. Serve on low-calorie, whole-wheat hamburger buns or English muffins.

"These bring back so may memories of being a kid! I'm pretty sure I ate these at every family picnic and also wore them home on my shirt. Try these with the Butternut Squash Fries (pg. 93)!"

Nutritional Value
Nutritional information is based on ⅓ cup.

Calories: 100   Fat: 4g   Carbohydrates: 4g   Protein: 11g   Sugar: 2g

greek turkey burger

Makes 5 servings.

INGREDIENTS

- 1   lb. ground turkey or ground beef (93/7)
- ¼   c. kalamata olives, finely diced, finely diced
- ¼   c. green olives with pimento
- ¼   c. onion, diced
- ¼   c. walnuts, chopped
- ¼   c. fat-free feta cheese
- ¼   tsp. each of garlic powder, dried oregano and dried dill weed

   salt and pepper to taste

INSTRUCTIONS

1.   Mix all ingredients together and make into 5 equal patties.

2.   Grill until patties are completely cooked through.

3.   Serve on your favorite whole-grain hamburger bun or English muffin. Mix together fat-free Greek yogurt, a pinch of dried oregano and dill weed for a delicious topping for the burger.

4.   Top off with a slice of tomato.

> *"This mouth-watering burger is enough to bring a tear to my eye! I have a true love for olives. So this combination is heaven on a bun!"*

Nutritional Value
Nutritional information is based on 1 patty.

Calories: 201   Fat: 12g   Carbohydrates: 5g   Protein: 19g   Sugar: <1g

italian turkey burger

Makes 4 to 5 servings.

INGREDIENTS

- 1 tsp. fennel, chopped or crushed
- 1 Tbsp. minced garlic
- 16 oz. ground turkey/chicken/beef
- ½ c. onions, chopped
- ½ c. fresh parsley or 1 Tbsp. dried parsley
- ½ c. mushrooms, chopped
- 3 egg whites
- ½ c. Whole-Wheat Bread Crumbs, *pg. 163*
  - salt and pepper to taste
- ¼ tsp. red pepper
- 1 tsp. Italian seasoning
  - If desired for topping — light ricotta cheese, slice of light mozzarella or asiago cheese

INSTRUCTIONS

1. Pre-heat the grill.
2. Mix all ingredients together and form 4 to 5 patties.
3. Dance in place while burgers are grilling to burn extra calories.
4. For extra flavor, add low-sugar pizza sauce and 1 Tbsp. asiago cheese, slice light mozzarella or a dollop of light ricotta to patty while warm.
5. Serve on buns of choice (try Ezekiel® Buns) and bam! Italian burgers.

> *"Have it your way! Fabulous with toppings or alone.*
> *The flavors are drool worthy!"*

Nutritional Value
Nutritional information is based on 1 burger.

Calories: 206 Fat: 8g Carbohydrates: 4g Protein: 26g Sugar: 1g

italian turkey sausage

Makes 5 servings.

INGREDIENTS

16	oz. lean ground turkey
2	tsp. olive oil, if desired
½	tsp. garlic powder
3	Tbsp. Italian seasoning
3	Tbsp. fennel seed
½	tsp. red pepper flakes
2	tsp. smokey paprika
¼	tsp. ground cayenne pepper (optional)
	salt and pepper to taste

INSTRUCTIONS

1. Heat olive oil in a frying pan. Add the ground turkey and all seasonings.

2. Cook until well done. Chop turkey while frying to hamburger consistency.

"This was the very first recipe on my website! It is an absolute staple in my house every week. It's also one of my ultimate favorite things to eat and is the base of many recipes I make. Keep this in your house and toss it into anything you can think of to add some lean protein and hefty flavor! Everyone loves this recipe!"

hint:

This recipe can be doubled or tripled, packaged in desired serving sizes and frozen. Can use this low-calorie, low-fat recipe in place of any ground sausage in any recipe.

Nutritional Value

Nutritional information is based on ½ cup.

Calories: 106   Fat: 16g   Carbohydrates: <1g   Protein: 17g   Sugar: <1g

turkey chili

Makes 10 servings.

INGREDIENTS

2	lbs. ground turkey
1	medium onion, diced
1	Tbsp. minced garlic
1	28 oz. can crushed tomatoes
2	15 oz. cans diced tomatoes with chilies
4	Tbsp. tomato paste
1	bottle of light beer
15	oz. can beef broth
2	Tbsp. each of ground cumin and chili powder
1	tsp. each of cocoa powder and dried oregano
2	bay leaves
7	packets stevia or ¼ c. sugar
2	15 oz. cans great northern or navy beans
4	oz. whole-wheat spaghetti – broken into 2-inch pieces and cooked (feel free to sub your favorite healthy pasta or brown rice) salt and pepper to taste

INSTRUCTIONS

1. Brown ground turkey and onions until turkey is fully cooked. Add garlic and cook 1 minute more.

2. Add beer, crushed tomatoes, diced tomatoes with chilies, tomato paste, beef broth, bay leaves, cumin, chili powder, cocoa and oregano. Mix well. Stir in beans, cooked spaghetti and sweetener.

3. Simmer for 30 minutes. Remove bay leaves.

hint:

The secret to great chili is to build a multi-level of flavor. The beer and cocoa powder add a wonderfully complex flavor combined with the rest of the ingredients. This chili is tasty, healthy, low calorie and filling! This chili goes wonderfully with sweet corn bread. (See Sweet Corn Bread recipe at www.busygirlhealthylife.com/recipes.)

Nutritional Value
Nutritional information is based on 1½ cup.

Calories: 309 ❀ Fat: 7g ❀ Carbohydrates: 22g ❀ Protein: 24g ❀ Sugar: 7g

cheesy sausage and cauliflower casserole

Makes 16 servings.

INGREDIENTS

1   medium/large head of cauliflower

1   8 oz. package fresh baby bella mushrooms, diced

1   medium sweet onion, diced

1½   c. celery, diced

1   c. + ¼ c. low-fat sharp cheddar cheese

1   c. Italian Turkey Sausage, *pg. 121* (or ground turkey/chicken sausage of your choice), cooked

1   c. fat-free or low-fat plain Greek yogurt

1   tsp. garlic powder

     salt and pepper to taste

INSTRUCTIONS

1.   Preheat oven to 400 degrees.

2.   Cut fresh cauliflower into florets, stems removed. In large bowl, mix cauliflower, mushrooms, onion and celery, and mix with 1 Tbsp. olive oil.

3.   Transfer to baking sheet and roast for 25-30 minutes or until tender crisp.

4.   Remove from oven, transfer to a 9 x 13-inch baking dish.

5.   Stir together yogurt, 1 c. cheese, sausage and garlic powder.

6.   Pour on top of cauliflower mixture and mix well. Salt and pepper to taste.

7.   Sprinkle with remaining cheese, put back in oven and bake for 15-20 minutes until bubbly.

8.   Allow to cool for five minutes before serving.

Nutritional Value
Nutritional information is based on 1/2 cup.

Calories: 80 • Fat: 2g • Sodium: 200mg • Carbohydrates: 6g • Fiber: 2g • Sugar: 3g • Protein: 8g

chinese casserole

Makes 6 servings.

INGREDIENTS

- ¾ c. brown rice, uncooked
- 2 c. low-sodium beef broth
- 1 lb. ground turkey (93/7)
- 1 c. sweet onion, diced
- 1½ c. celery, diced
- 8 oz. can water chestnuts, diced
- 2 c. finely shredded cabbage
- ⅓-½ c. low-sodium soy sauce
- 1 Tbsp. hoisin sauce
- 2 tsp. toasted sesame oil
- ½ tsp. garlic powder
- salt and pepper to taste

INSTRUCTIONS

1. Cook rice according to package directions in 1½ c. beef broth.

2. While rice is cooking, brown turkey, celery, onion, water chestnuts and cabbage in a large nonstick frying pan until turkey is cooked through.

3. Add cooked rice to turkey mixture and mix well.

4. Add remaining beef broth, soy sauce, garlic powder, hoisin sauce and sesame oil to casserole. Mix well and cook until liquid is absorbed.

> *"I am a sucker for this casserole. The only problem I have with it is sharing! This sweet, spicy, crunchy dish covers any craving I'm having!"*

Nutritional Value
Nutritional information is based on about 1 cup.

Calories: 266 ❀ Fat: 7g ❀ Carbohydrates: 26g ❀ Protein: 18g ❀ Sugar: 4g

turkey stuffing

Makes 20 servings.

INGREDIENTS

- 2 c. celery, finely diced
- 1½ c. onion, finely diced
- 2 6.5 oz. cans mushroom stems and pieces, drained and diced
- 8 oz. can water chestnuts, drained and diced
- 6 c. herb-seasoned stuffing bread crumbs
- 1½ c. Italian Turkey Sausage, *pg. 121*
- 4 Tbsp. light butter, melted
- ⅔ c. low-fat buttermilk
- 4 c. low-sodium chicken stock

  salt and pepper to taste

INSTRUCTIONS

1. Preheat oven to 350 degrees.
2. Mix all ingredients together. Let sit for 1 hour so all flavors blend.
3. Transfer to a large casserole dish sprayed with nonstick cooking spray.
4. Bake for 45 minutes or until light crust forms on top of casserole.

> *"My holidays never go without this staple! Try it out and see why I don't need a nap after our feast — so delicious and healthy! Great complement to any ham or turkey dish."*

Nutritional Value
Nutritional information is based on ½ cup.

Calories: 87 ✸ Fat: 4g ✸ Carbohydrates: 11g ✸ Protein: 5g ✸ Sugar: 2g

veggie stuffing

Makes 20 servings.

INGREDIENTS

1	c. onion, finely diced
1½	c. celery, finely diced
8	oz. fresh mini bella mushrooms, diced
8	oz. can water chestnuts, drained and diced
2	c. frozen chopped broccoli, thawed
2	c. frozen cauliflower, thawed and diced
1½	c. Italian Turkey Sausage, *pg. 121*
1	c. Whole-Wheat Bread Crumbs, *pg. 163*
1	c. fat-free cottage cheese
¼	c. grated Parmesan cheese
2	Tbsp. light butter, melted
½	c. low-fat buttermilk
½	tsp. ground poultry seasoning
¼	tsp. garlic powder
1	c. low-sodium chicken stock
	salt and pepper to taste

INSTRUCTIONS

1. Preheat oven to 350 degrees.

2. Mix all ingredients together. Let sit 1 hour so all flavors blend.
   Transfer to a large casserole dish sprayed with nonstick cooking spray.

3. Bake for 45 minutes or until light crust forms on top of casserole.

Recipe can be cut in half. Freezes well.

> *"This is one of my absolute favorite things to eat!*
> *I could eat this as a meal in itself."*

Nutritional Value
Nutritional information is based on about ½ cup.

Calories: 53   ❀   Fat: 2g   ❀   Carbohydrates: 4g   ❀   Protein: 6g   ❀   Sugar: 2g

skinny pigs in a blanket

Makes 4 servings.

INGREDIENTS

4   sheets phyllo dough

4   smoked turkey sausages, turkey dogs
     or vegetarian dogs

     butter-flavored cooking spray

INSTRUCTIONS

1. Preheat oven to 400 degrees.

2. Roll out 4 sheets of phyllo dough and quarter
    them with a pizza cutter.

3. Spray 2 of the quartered sheets with cooking
    spray. Put 2 more quartered sheets on top
    of sprayed sheets and spray top with cooking spray.

4. Place 1 sausage or hot dog in sprayed sheets and roll up. Spray top of roll.

5. Place on a cookie sheet coated with cooking spray. Bake for 10 to 12 minutes
    or until dough is lightly brown and crisp.

Dip in your favorite sauces!

> *"These are a fun, easy appetizer or meal for kids or at any party!
> Try dipping them in one of my dressings in the cookbook! Kid
> tested, husband approved!"*

Nutritional Value
Nutritional information is based on 1 pig in the blanket.

Calories: 143   Fat: 6g   Carbohydrates: 10g   Protein: 11g   Sugar: 2g

pumpkin sausage penne

Makes 8 servings.

INGREDIENTS

1	lb. Italian Turkey Sausage, (about 2½ cups), *pg. 121*
1	medium diced onion
2	Tbsp. minced garlic
4	oz. canned sliced mushrooms
¾	c. white wine
1	c. chicken broth
15	oz. can plain pumpkin
¼	tsp. each ground sage and dried thyme
½	c. low-fat buttermilk
12	oz. box whole-wheat penne, cooked
⅓	c. grated Parmesan cheese

INSTRUCTIONS

1. In large pan, sauté mushrooms and onions until onions are translucent.

2. Add garlic and cook for one more minute. Add cooked turkey sausage, white wine, chicken broth, pumpkin, sage, thyme, nutmeg and stir.

3. Add buttermilk, cheese and cooked penne. Mix well.

4. Simmer on low heat for 15 minutes.

"This is my 'fool your husband into eating healthy' dish! He will never know it's not the rich restaurant alternative! Keep your heart and stomach happy."

hint:

Try subbing 12 oz. cooked spaghetti squash for a cleaner dish.

Nutritional Value
Nutritional information is based on about ⅛ of pasta dish.

Calories: 275 ❀ Fat: 5g ❀ Carbohydrates: 32g ❀ Protein: 19g ❀ Sugar: 5g

lean, mean and green goulash

Makes 6 servings.

INGREDIENTS

1   lb. extra-lean ground beef or ground turkey
½   green bell pepper, chopped
½   red bell pepper, chopped
1   c. onion, chopped
2   garlic cloves, chopped
⅛   tsp. red pepper flakes
1   can whole tomatoes with juice
2   Tbsp. tomato paste
1   tsp. ground basil
4   zucchini squashes, chopped
1   Tbsp. olive oil

INSTRUCTIONS

1. Preheat oven to 350 degrees. In a sauté pan over medium heat, combine all ingredients through the red pepper flakes and cook until beef/turkey is no longer pink.

2. While the meat mixture is cooking, sauté chopped zucchini in a saucepan over medium heat until soft. Add tomatoes through basil to meat mixture and bring to a simmer.

3. Combine meat mixture and zucchini in an oven-safe pan and bake, covered with foil, for 30 minutes or until edges are golden brown.

4. Serve warm and ENJOY!

Nutritional Value
Nutritional information is based on 1/6 of recipe.

Calories: 163 ❀ Fat: 5g ❀ Sodium: 190mg ❀ Carbohydrates: 12g ❀ Fiber: 3g ❀ Sugar: 6g ❀ Protein: 17g

balsamic filet mignon

Makes 4 servings.

INGREDIENTS

4	4 oz. tenderloin fillets
1	Tbsp. olive oil
2	Tbsp. light butter
2-3	shallots, finely diced
½	c. red wine
½	c. good-quality balsamic vinegar
¼	tsp. cocoa powder
1	clove garlic, finely diced
4	oz. fresh baby bella mushrooms, sliced
	salt and pepper to taste

INSTRUCTIONS

1. Pat steaks dry, and salt and pepper to taste.

2. Preheat skillet on medium-high heat, and melt oil and 1 Tbsp. butter in skillet.

3. Add tenderloins, sear for 4 minutes, then flip fillets and sear other side for 4 minutes. Remove steaks from heat.

4. In same skillet, add last tablespoon butter, shallots and mushrooms, and sauté until mushrooms brown.

5. Add garlic, wine, vinegar and cocoa powder and bring to boil. Add salt and pepper to taste and turn down heat and simmer until liquid reduces by half.

6. Add steaks to pan and cook until desired doneness (2-3 minutes each side for medium rare or 3-5 minutes each side for medium well).

7. Remove steaks from pan, cover with foil and let rest for 10 minutes.

8. Spoon sauce reduction over steaks and serve.

Nutritional Value
Nutritional information is based on 1 tenderloin or 1/4 of recipe.

Calories: 395 ● Fat: 26g ● Sodium: 390mg ● Carbohydrates: 7g ● Fiber: 1g ● Sugar: 1g ● Protein: 31g

mushroom swiss burger

Makes 5 servings.

INGREDIENTS

- 1 lb. ground turkey (93/7)
  or ground sirloin (93/7)
- 6 oz. chopped portobello mushrooms
- ½ c. diced onion
- 5 wedges of Laughing Cow® Light Swiss Cheese
  (partially frozen for easy chopping)
- 1-1½ Tbsp. Worcestershire sauce
- ¼ tsp. garlic powder
- salt and pepper to taste

INSTRUCTIONS

1. Dice frozen cheese.
2. Sauté mushrooms in nonstick skillet until lightly brown.
3. Mix all ingredients together and make into 5 equal patties.
4. Grill until patties are completely cooked through.
5. Serve on your favorite whole-grain hamburger bun or English muffin.

> *"This is a serious sandwich that will make any
> burger-lover a believer! Such a fun spin on grilling out!"*

Nutritional Value
Nutritional information is based on 1 patty.

Calories: 190 ❖ Fat: 8g ❖ Carbohydrates: 4g ❖ Protein: 20g ❖ Sugar: 2g

blue cheese-crusted tenderloin filet

Makes 4 servings.

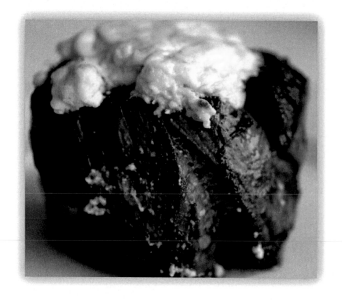

INGREDIENTS

4	4 oz. tenderloin fillets
⅓	c. low-fat crumbled blue cheese
½	c. Whole-Wheat Bread Crumbs, *pg. 163*
¼	tsp. garlic salt
⅛	tsp. cayenne pepper
1	Tbsp. chopped fresh basil
	salt and pepper to taste

INSTRUCTIONS

1. Preheat oven to 450 degrees.

2. Combine cheese, bread crumbs, garlic salt, cayenne and basil in mixing bowl. Set aside.

3. Spray oven-proof skillet with cooking spray. Generously season fillets with salt and pepper.

4. Sear first side of steak for about 2 minutes until well browned. Flip steak and top each with ¼ of cheese mixture, pressing gently into meat.

5. Put steaks in oven and bake for 6 to 7 minutes or until they feel firm but springy to the touch. Steaks should be medium rare. If medium is desired, cook steaks for another 1 to 2 minutes. Cheese mixture will be lightly browned and crusted.

6. Let steaks rest for a few minutes before serving.

Nutritional Value
Nutritional information is based on 1 fillet.

Calories: 203   Fat: 9g   Carbohydrates: 2g   Protein: 27g   Sugar: <1g

philly cheesesteak quesadilla

Makes 2 servings.

INGREDIENTS

4	oz. raw tenderloin, cut into thin strips
4	oz. fresh baby bella mushrooms, sliced
1	medium sweet onion, sliced
1	medium red bell pepper, sliced
½	c. shredded, low-fat mozzarella cheese
¼	tsp. garlic salt, divided
	pinch of dried thyme leaves
2	large whole-wheat, low-carb tortilla

INSTRUCTIONS

1. In a hot, nonstick pan coated with nonstick cooking spray, sauté all ingredients, except tortillas and cheese, until steak and veggies are tender. Salt and pepper to taste.

2. Put half of the steak mixture on half of each tortilla. Cover each steak mixture with half of the cheese.

3. Fold each tortilla over and cook in nonstick pan coated with cooking spray until bottom of tortillas are lightly brown and crisp.

4. Spray top of tortillas with cooking spray and flip them over in the pan. Cook for 2 to 4 minutes or until that side is lightly brown and crisp.

Nutritional Value
Nutritional information is based on 1 quesadilla.

Calories: 278　　Fat: 10g　　Carbohydrates: 16g　　Protein: 29g　　Sugar: 5g

pork tenderloin chops

Makes 4 servings.

INGREDIENTS

- 4   4 oz. boneless pork tenderloin chops
- ½   c. low-fat buttermilk
- 1   c. Whole-Wheat Bread Crumbs, *pg. 163*
- 2   tsp. dijon mustard
- ¼   tsp. each garlic powder, onion powder and ground sage
  - salt and pepper to taste

INSTRUCTIONS

1. Preheat oven to 375 degrees.

2. Marinate tenderloins in buttermilk and mustard for 1 hour or overnight.

3. Mix bread crumbs with garlic powder, onion powder and sage.

4. Dredge tenderloins in bread crumbs and put on a baking sheet sprayed with cooking spray. Salt and pepper to taste. Spray top of tenderloins with cooking spray.

5. Bake in oven for 20 to 25 minutes, or until light pink inside, flipping chops halfway through baking time.

Nutritional Value
Nutritional information is based on 1 chop.

Calories: 181   Fat: 4g   Carbohydrates: 6g   Protein: 27g   Sugar: 3g

eggplant parmigiana

Makes 8 servings.

INGREDIENTS

- 1 medium eggplant
- 2 large egg whites
- ¼ c. low-fat buttermilk
- 1-1½ c. Whole-Wheat Bread Crumbs, *pg. 163*
- ½ tsp. Italian seasoning
- ¾ tsp. each onion powder and garlic powder, divided
- ½ c. low-fat shredded mozzarella cheese
- ½ c. shredded Parmesan
- 1 15 oz. can crushed tomatoes
- ½ tsp. each cayenne pepper and red pepper flakes
- 2-3 packets of stevia or 4 tsp. sugar

INSTRUCTIONS

1. Preheat oven to 425 degrees.

2. Whisk together egg whites, buttermilk and ¼ tsp. each of the onion and garlic powder.

3. In separate bowl, mix bread crumbs, ¼ tsp. each onion and garlic powder, and Italian seasoning.

4. Peel and slice eggplant into 8 slices lengthwise.

5. Dip eggplant in egg mixture, and then dredge in bread crumbs, patting down to make sure eggplant is completely covered.

6. Put eggplant on an 11 x 16 jelly roll pan sprayed with cooking spray.

7. Spray top of eggplant with cooking spray and bake for 20 to 25 minutes. Turn eggplant halfway through cooking time.

8. While eggplant is baking, simmer tomatoes, ¼ tsp. each onion and garlic powder, Italian seasoning, cayenne pepper, red pepper flakes and sweetener on stove top for 10 minutes.

9. Spread tomato sauce over eggplant, sprinkle with mozzarella and Parmesan cheeses.

10. Return to oven and bake about 5 minutes or until cheese melts.

> *"A family favorite for dinner and leftovers! Anything that ends in 'parmigiana' has to be amazing! Your mouth will be singing 'That's amoré' in no time. Just remember, chew first and sing later!"*

Nutritional Value

Nutritional information is based on 1 slice eggplant and ⅛ of sauce

Calories: 100 ❋ Fat: 3g ❋ Carbohydrates: 9g ❋ Protein: 8g ❋ Sugar: 3g

fish & seafood

cayenne lime shrimp

Makes about 31 to 40 servings.

INGREDIENTS

1   lb. (31-40 count) frozen raw shrimp,
    thawed, peeled and deveined

2   Tbsp. lime juice

2   tsp. light olive oil

½   tsp. cayenne pepper

½   tsp. garlic salt

INSTRUCTIONS

1. Rinse shrimp. Combine all ingredients
    and marinate in refrigerator for 30 minutes.

2. Remove shrimp from marinade and grill
    2 to 3 minutes on each side until shrimp
    is tender and cooked through. Do not
    over cook.

"Throw another shrimp on the barbie! These shrimp are the perfect party starter, and also go perfectly on any skewer or salad."

Nutritional Value
Nutritional information is based on 1 cooked shrimp.

Calories: 11   Fat: <1g   Carbohydrates: 0g   Protein: 2g   Sugar: 0g

coconut shrimp

Makes 31-40 coconut shrimp.

INGREDIENTS

1	lb. (31-40 count) frozen, shelled and deveined raw shrimp, thawed
1	c. panko bread crumbs
½	c. whole-wheat flour
½	c. unsweetened shredded coconut
½	Whole-Wheat Bread Crumbs, *pg. 163*
3	egg whites
¼	tsp. cayenne pepper
2	packets stevia or 1 Tbsp. sugar
2-3	3 Tbsp. water
	salt and pepper to taste

INSTRUCTIONS

1. Preheat oven to 375 degrees.
2. Put flour, salt and pepper in large plastic bag. Shake bag. Add shrimp and shake until shrimp is coated with flour.
3. Put panko, coconut, cayenne, sweetener, salt and pepper in a large shallow bowl and mix well.
4. In separate bowl, whisk egg whites with water.
5. Working with a few shrimp at a time, dip floured shrimp in egg wash. Then put shrimp into coconut mixture and roll around until shrimp are thoroughly covered.
6. Place breaded shrimp on nonstick baking sheet and bake for 10 minutes or until shrimp are firm and cooked through.

Goes great with jalapeño coconut rice.

> ### *Asian Dipping Sauce:*
> *Whisk 2 Tbsp. Asian sweet chili dipping sauce with 2 Tbsp. low-sodium chicken sauce for a tasty addition — only 45 Calories!*

Nutritional Value
Nutritional information is based on 1 shrimp.

Calories: 37 　Fat: 1g 　Carbohydrates: 4g 　Protein: 4g 　Sugar: <1g

maple pecan salmon

Makes 8 servings

let

INGREDIENTS

¼ c. natural maple syrup

¼ c. fat-free or low fat plain Greek yogurt

1 Tbsp. dijon mustard

1 tsp. salt

½ tsp. pepper

¾ c. plain panko bread crumbs

½ c. pecans, finely chopped

8 4-5 oz. boneless, skinless salmon

INSTRUCTIONS

1. Preheat oven to 400 degrees.

2. Mix together syrup, yogurt, mustard salt and pepper. Put salmon in large plastic bag and pour syrup mixture over salmon and marinate in refrigerator for 1 hour.

3. Mix together the panko bread crumbs and pecans. Take salmon out of marinade and dredge into panko mixture until coated.

4. Put salmon on a baking sheet and bake for 20 minutes or until salmon is baked to desired doneness.

5. Change oven to broil and broil salmon until top is brown and crisp (about 1-2 minutes). Watch closely so as not to burn the top.

6. Remove and place on serving tray!

Nutritional Value
Nutritional information is based on 1 salmon fillet or 1/8 of recipe.

Calories: 315 ● Fat: 16g ● Sodium: 450mg ● Carbohydrates: 15g ● Fiber: 1g ● Sugar: 7g ● Protein: 28g

asian salmon

Makes 4 servings

INGREDIENTS

4	4 oz. skinless salmon
⅓	c. low-sodium soy sauce
⅓	c. orange juice
¼	c. natural maple syrup
1	tsp. sesame oil
¼-½	tsp. ground ginger
¼	tsp. garlic powder
	salt and pepper to taste

INSTRUCTIONS

1. Preheat oven to 400 degrees.

2. Mix all ingredients except salmon in oven-proof baking dish.

3. Add salmon and flip in sauce until completely covered. Marinate for 20 minutes.

4. Bake salmon in sauce for 15 to 20 minutes, flipping halfway through (periodically basting fillets), until fish is cooked to medium to medium-well depending on preference.

5. Pour any remaining sauce over salmon before serving.

Nutritional Value
Nutritional information is based on 1 fillet.

Calories: 169   Fat: 5g   Carbohydrates: 6g   Protein: 25g   Sugar: 2g

crunchy fish sticks

Fish Sticks
Makes 4 servings.
Tarter Sauce
Makes ¾ c. (12 Tbsp.)

INGREDIENTS

Fish Sticks

- 1 lb. white fish (haddock, cod, tilapia or flounder)
- 1 c. Whole-Wheat Bread Crumbs, *pg. 163*
- ½ c. whole-wheat flour
- 3 egg whites, beaten
- ⅛ tsp. each garlic and onion powder
   salt and pepper to taste

Tarter Sauce

- ½ c. fat-free Greek yogurt
- 2 Tbsp. low-fat mayo
- 1 tsp. mustard
- 2 Tbsp. sweet pickle relish
- 1 tsp. vinegar
- 1 packet stevia or 2 tsp. sugar
   salt to taste.

INSTRUCTIONS

1. Preheat oven to 400 degrees.

2. Cut fish into 4- by 1-inch sticks.

3. Put flour into plastic bag, and add salt and pepper to taste. Add fish sticks to bag and shake well until sticks are covered with flour.

4. Mix bread crumbs and spices (including salt and pepper), and stir well.

5. Dredge floured sticks in beaten egg whites, then in bread crumb mixture, making sure fish is well covered.

6. Place breaded fish sticks on pre-sprayed baking sheet. Bake for 10 to 15 minutes until fish is done.

7. Mix tarter sauce ingredients together.

8. Add a splash of skim milk if sauce is too thick.

> *"These are so quick and fun to make with your kids!*
> *If you can't have shore lunch, this is the next best thing!"*

Nutritional Value
Nutritional information is based on ¼ of fish sticks (about 4 to 6 sticks).

Calories: 194   Fat: 1g   Carbohydrates: 14g   Protein: 28g   Sugar: 1g

Tarter Sauce
Calories: 11   Fat: <1g   Carbohydrates: 1g   Protein: 1g   Sugar: 1g

fish tacos

Makes 8 servings.

INGREDIENTS

1½ lbs. mild white fish
(haddock, cod, tilapia, etc.)
8 whole-wheat soft tortillas
(warmed or cooked in frying pan
with olive oil spray – 1 minute each side)

Marinade

2 Tbsp. fresh lime juice
1 tsp. olive oil
½ tsp. cumin
½ tsp. paprika,
½ tsp. garlic powder

Coleslaw

1 bag shredded cabbage (about 4 cups)
½ c. green onion, chopped
1 to 2 Tbsp. finely chopped jalapeño
1 Tbsp. fresh cilantro, chopped
3 Tbsp. white wine vinegar
2 Tbsp. fresh lime juice
1 tsp. celery salt
2 Tbsp. olive oil
3 Tbsp. fat-free Greek yogurt
½ tsp. garlic powder
6 packets stevia or ¼ c. sugar

Cucumber/Corn Salsa

2 c. cucumbers, diced
2 Roma tomatoes, finely diced
1 c. corn
¼ c. green onion, diced
1 Tbsp. finely diced jalapeño
1 Tbsp. fresh cilantro, chopped
2 Tbsp. fresh lime juice
½ tsp. ground cumin
½ tsp. garlic powder
2 tsp. olive oil
1 packet stevia or 2 tsp. sugar
salt and pepper to taste

INSTRUCTIONS

1. Marinate fish in marinade, set aside.

2. Preheat oven to 375 degrees.

3. While fish is marinating, in large bowl beat together white wine vinegar, lime juice, celery salt, olive oil, yogurt, garlic powder and sweetener from coleslaw recipe. Add cabbage, green onion, jalapeño and cilantro. Mix well and set aside.

4. Bake fish for 10 to 12 minutes or until fish is done.

5. While fish is baking, mix together salsa ingredients.

6. When fish is done, pull fish apart with forks to roughly shred. To prepare tacos, put coleslaw in wrap, followed by some fish and top with the salsa.

Nutritional Value
Nutritional information is based on 1 taco.

Calories: 250 ❀ Fat: 9g ❀ Carbohydrates: 13g ❀ Protein: 27g ❀ Sugar: 5g

seafood enchiladas

Makes 8 servings.

INGREDIENTS

12	oz. crab (can use imitation crab), diced
12	oz. cooked shrimp, finely diced
⅔	c. low-fat buttermilk
1	c. fat-free cottage cheese
1	c. fat-free ricotta cheese
1	c. low-fat monterey cheese, shredded
1	medium red onion
1	Tbsp. corn starch
¾	c. salsa verde, divided
8	whole-wheat, low-carb large tortillas
1	packet stevia or 2 tsp. sugar

INSTRUCTIONS

1. Preheat oven to 375 degrees.

2. Sauté onions, in nonstick pan until tender.

3. Add cottage cheese, monterey cheese, crab, shrimp and ¼ c. salsa verde. Cook until cheese melts and seafood is well blended. Salt and pepper to taste.

4. In separate pan, heat ½ c. salsa, buttermilk, corn starch, sweetener and ricotta cheese until bubbly and cheese is melted. Salt and pepper to taste.

5. Fill tortilla with ⅛ of seafood mixture and roll tortilla. Repeat with other 7 tortillas.

6. Put in a baking dish sprayed with cooking spray. Cover tortillas with salsa mixture.

7. Bake in oven for 20 to 25 minutes until bubbly.

Nutritional Value
Nutritional information is based on 1 enchilada.

Calories: 270 ✤ Fat: 7g ✤ Carbohydrates: 13g ✤ Protein: 32g ✤ Sugar: 4g

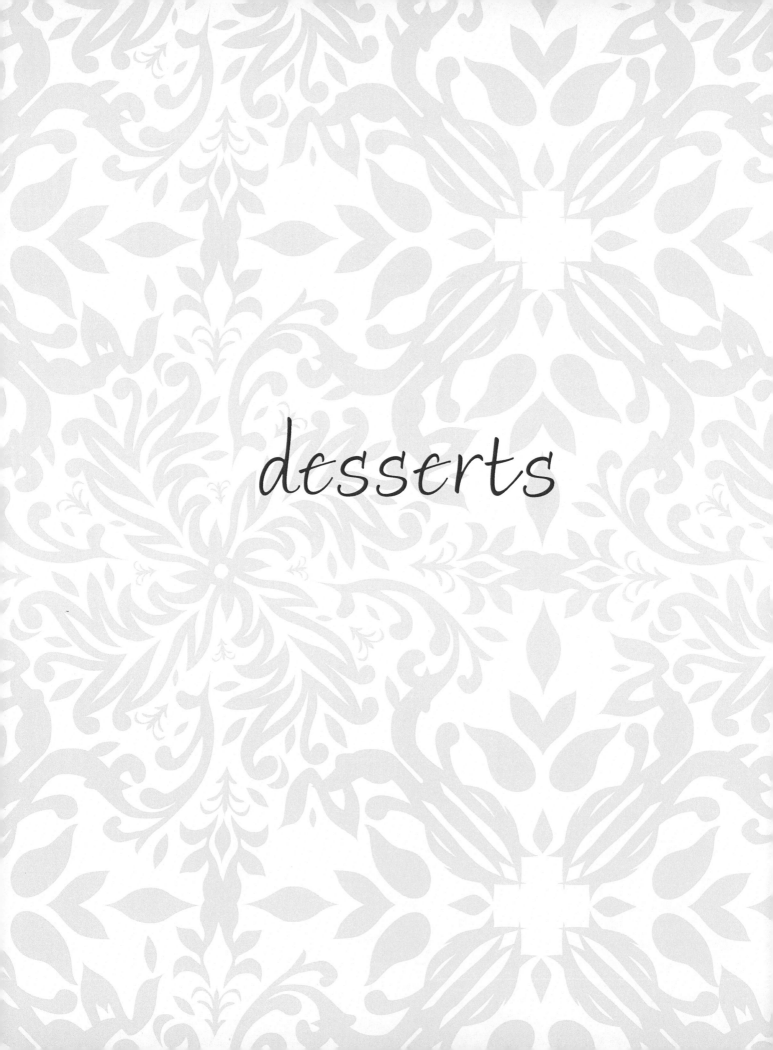

desserts

chocolate pecan coconut meringues

Makes 3 dozen cookies.

INGREDIENTS

- 3 large egg whites, room temperature
- ⅛ tsp. cream of tartar
- 1 tsp. vanilla
- 2 Tbsp. unsweetened cocoa powder, sifted
- ⅓-½ c. coconut sugar
- ⅓ c. pecans, finely chopped
- ¼ c. unsweetened coconut flakes

INSTRUCTIONS

1. Preheat oven to 300 degrees. Line baking sheet with parchment paper.

2. In mixing bowl, beat egg whites and cream of tartar to a soft peak consistency.

3. While continuing to beat slowly, add sugar and vanilla until mixture reaches a stiff peak consistency.

4. Slowly fold in the cocoa powder, pecans and coconut flakes until well blended. Do not over mix.

5. Spoon a tablespoon of mixture onto parchment paper-lined baking sheet.

6. Bake for 30-35 minutes.

Nutritional Value
Nutritional information is based on 1 cookie

Calories: 20   Fat: 1g   Sodium: 5mg   Carbohydrates: 3g   Fiber: 0g   Sugar: 2g   Protein: 0g

maple-pecan pear tartlets

Makes 15 tartlets.

INGREDIENTS

15	mini phyllo shells
1	ripe pear, peeled, cored and finely diced
½	c. chopped pecans
1½	Tbsp. maple syrup
1	egg white
¼	tsp. vanilla
⅛-¼	tsp. cinnamon
	pinch of salt

INSTRUCTIONS

1. Preheat oven to 375 degrees.

2. In a mixing bowl, beat egg white, vanilla, maple syrup, cinnamon and salt together. Stir in pears and pecans until well blended.

3. Fill shells with pecan mixture and put shells in mini muffin pan (so shells hold their shape).

4. Bake for 20 minutes.

Nutritional Value
Nutritional information is based on 1 tartlet.

Calories: 50   Fat: 3g   Sodium: 20mg   Carbohydrates: 4g   Fiber: 1g   Sugar: 3g   Protein: 1g

pumpkin cheesecake soufflé

Makes 8 soufflés.

INGREDIENTS

1	8 oz. block of light cream cheese, room temperature
1	c. pumpkin puree
⅔	c. fat-free Greek yogurt, room temperature
⅓	c. coconut sugar
¼	tsp. vanilla
½	tsp. pumpkin pie spice
3	egg whites, room temperature
⅛	tsp. cream of tartar
2	Tbsp. coconut sugar
1	tsp. light butter

INSTRUCTIONS

1. Preheat oven to 375 degrees.

2. Coat 8 ramekins with light butter. Place cups on baking sheet and set aside.

3. In a mixing bowl, beat cream cheese, pumpkin, yogurt, 1/3 c. coconut sugar, pumpkin pie spice and vanilla until well blended.

4. In medium mixing bowl, beat egg whites and cream of tarter with electric mixer until soft peaks form. Slowly add 2 Tbsp. sugar and continue to beat until stiff peaks form.

5. Gently fold egg white mixture into pumpkin mixture until white streaks disappear. Do not over stir.

6. Evenly divide mixture into prepared cups and bake for 15 minutes until soufflés are puffed and knife gently inserted in center comes out clean.

7. Gently remove from oven and serve.

Nutritional Value
Nutritional information is based on 1 soufflé.

Calories: 145   Fat: 6g   Sodium: 170mg   Carbohydrates: 16g   Fiber: 1g   Sugar: 15g   Protein: 6g

moist pumpkin muffins

Makes 12 servings.

INGREDIENTS

Submitted by Heather Riley of Florida

1	c. canned pumpkin
1/2	c. applesauce
1/2	c. plain low-fat Greek yogurt
3	egg whites
1¾	c. old-fashioned oats
¼	c. baking stevia
1	tsp. baking soda
2	tsp. baking powder
¼	tsp. salt
1½	tsp. cinnamon
½	tsp. pumpkin pie or apple pie spice

INSTRUCTIONS

1. Preheat oven to 350 degrees. Line a 12-cup muffin pan with foil cupcake liners and/or nonstick cooking spray. Set aside.

2. In a blender or food processor, mix all of the ingredients together. Blend until oats are ground and mixture is smooth. Use spoon to move mixture around if necessary between blending.

3. Divide mixture among muffin tins, and bake for 15-20 minutes, or until tops are lightly golden brown. Note: this batter is very moist, and toothpick may not come out clean. Don't worry, it's baked through if the tops are golden brown.

4. Cool muffins before removing from pan, and enjoy!

Nutritional Value
Nutritional information is based on 1 muffin.

Calories: 80   Fat: 2g   Sodium: 260mg   Carbohydrates: 18g   Fiber: 3g   Sugar: 5g   Protein: 4g

no-bake pb pumpkin balls

Makes about 30 mini balls.

INGREDIENTS

- 1 c. canned pumpkin
- ¾ c. gluten-free oats
- ½ c. oat flour (or make your own by blending oats in food processor)
- ½ tsp. cinnamon
- ¼ tsp. salt
- ¼ tsp. baking soda
- ¼ c. honey or you can substitute with 1½ Tbsp. stevia (3 packets) or ¼ c. brown sugar
- 3 Tbsp. powdered peanut butter OR 2 Tbsp. of your favorite nut or seed butter
- ⅓ c. canned pumpkin
- 1-2 Tbsp. of water if needed
- 1 Tbsp. olive oil or try adding your favorite nut oil such as hazelnut, walnut etc.
- ½ tsp. pure vanilla extract

INSTRUCTIONS

1. Preheat oven to 350 degrees. Line a 12-cup muffin pan with foil cupcake liners and/or nonstick cooking spray. Set aside.

2. Use two separate bowls for dry and wet ingredients.

3. Make sure you stir the dry ingredients in one bowl then mix well.

4. In the other bowl, be sure to mix all wet ingredients well.

5. Add wet ingredients to the dry and mix well.

6. You will need to refrigerate about 5–10 minutes before forming into mini balls.

7. Once mixture is cold, take out and hand roll into balls.

8. Place back in refrigerator until ready to serve.

9. These are fabulous frozen treats as well!

> *Try them frozen for a yummy treat!*

Nutritional Value
Nutritional information is based on 1 ball.

Calories: 32   Fat: 1g   Sodium: 35mg   Carbohydrates: 6g   Fiber: 1g   Sugar: 3g   Protein: 1g

awesomely autumn pumpkin dip

Makes 8 servings.

INGREDIENTS

- 1 c. canned pumpkin
- ¾ c. (6 oz). fat-free cream cheese, softened
- 6 packets stevia (1 Tbsp. + 2 tsp.)
- ½ c. canned pumpkin
- 1 Tbsp. maple syrup
- ½ tsp. ground cinnamon

INSTRUCTIONS

1. Combine all ingredients until smooth and chill for 20 to 30 minutes.

2. Serve with apple and pear slices or pita chips!

Nutritional Value
Nutritional information is based on 1/8 of recipe.

Calories: 66   Fat: 5g   Sodium: 90mg   Carbohydrates: 6g   Fiber: 1g   Sugar: 2g   Protein: 2g

chewy apple fro-yo

Makes 4 servings.

INGREDIENTS

2	c. fat-free Greek yogurt
4	apples, peeled and shredded
2	Tbsp. brown sugar
½	c. oatmeal
1	tsp. cinnamon
3-4	packets of stevia or 4 Tbsp. honey
1	tsp. vanilla
	pinch of salt

INSTRUCTIONS

1. Peel and shred apples, and place in a frying pan on medium heat. Cook until apples have created their own sauce and are quite soft (about 4 to 5 minutes).

2. Add 2 Tbsp. brown sugar and 1/2 cup oats to the pan and cook 3 to 4 more minutes until the oats are lightly toasted. Do not burn the brown sugar or let the apples get too dry. Take off heat and set aside.

3. Take 2 cups of yogurt and add cinnamon, vanilla, a tiny pinch of salt and stevia (or 4 Tbsp. of honey). Mix well.

4. Once apple mixture has cooled, add it to the yogurt and stir well.

5. Place in a large plastic container (with lid) and freeze. Will be ready to serve in 90 minutes. If you let it freeze for much longer, you will need to let it stand and warm up at room temperature for 5 to 10 minutes before scooping.

tips:

For best results, drizzle honey over the top of yogurt. For a more personal experience, freeze in 4 individual dishes. Feel free to add a sprinkle of oatmeal over the top as well!

Nutritional Value
Nutritional information is based on 1/4 of recipe.

Calories: 205   Fat: 1g   Sodium: 50mg   Carbohydrates: 40g   Fiber: 5g   Sugar: 26g   Protein: 13g

chocolate cheesecake bites

Makes about 15 servings.

INGREDIENTS

- 4   oz. fat-free cream cheese
- 4   oz. fat-free Greek yogurt
- 15 baked mini phyllo shells
- 6   packets stevia or ¼ c. sugar
- ½ tsp. vanilla
- 1   Tbsp. cocoa powder

  topping of choice or chocolate sprinkles (optional)

INSTRUCTIONS

1. Bring cream cheese and yogurt to room temperature.

2. Beat together cream cheese, yogurt, vanilla, cocoa powder and sweetener until creamy.

3. Fill phyllo shells full with cheese mixture. Sprinkle with chocolate sprinkles if desired.

4. Chill for 1 hour, and enjoy!

hint:

These freeze well. Make lots ahead of time and freeze. When you go to a party, simply take desired amount out of freezer, thaw and people will beg for the recipe! Always keep a supply on hand in the freezer. When you get that urge for something sweet, grab 1 or 2 and you will satisfy that craving without eating a lot of calories or fat.

"I've never met a chocolate dessert I didn't like! This is a party favorite, and aren't they just the cutest darn things? I love that they come in their own edible container and are the perfect bite-sized treat!"

Nutritional Value
Nutritional information is based on 1 cheesecake bite.

Calories: 31   Fat: 1g   Carbohydrates: 3g   Protein: 2g   Sugar: <1g

chocolate coffee soufflés

Makes about 6 servings.

INGREDIENTS

- ¼   c. unsweetened cocoa powder
- 1   Tbsp. instant coffee granules
- 2   Tbsp. cornstarch
- 1   tsp. ground cinnamon
- 2   packets stevia or 1 Tbsp. sugar
- ½   tsp. cream of tarter
- ¾   c. fat-free evaporated milk
- ½   c. natural maple syrup
- 3   egg whites, room temperature
- 2   egg yolks, room temperature

INSTRUCTIONS

1. Preheat oven to 400 degrees.
2. Coat six 6-ounce soufflé cups with cooking spray. Place cups on baking sheet.
3. In sauce pan, whisk together cocoa powder, instant coffee, cornstarch, sweetener and cinnamon. Stir in milk and maple syrup, and whisk over medium heat until hot (about 4 to 8 minutes).
4. In small bowl, whisk egg yolks lightly. Slowly whisk in ½ c. of cocoa mixture.
5. Pour into the saucepan and mix well.
6. In a large bowl, with an electric mixer, beat egg whites and cream of tartar on high until soft peaks form.
7. Gently stir ⅓ of egg white into cocoa mixture. Fold in remaining egg whites until no white streaks remain. Do not over stir.
8. Evenly divide mixture into prepared cups and bake for 15 to 20 minutes until soufflés are puffed, and a knife inserted in center comes out clean. Serve immediately.

"These are perfect for when I am having a crazy chocolate craving! Make sure you have enough people to help you eat these so you don't eat the whole batch!"

Nutritional Value
Nutritional information is based on 1 soufflé.

Calories: 79   Fat: 2g   Carbohydrates: 10g   Protein: 5g   Sugar: 4g

chewy chocolate brownies

Makes 12 servings.

INGREDIENTS

1¼   c. whole-wheat pastry flour

1½   tsp. baking powder

½   tsp. salt

⅔   c. unsweetened cocoa powder

16   packets stevia or ¾ c. sugar

5   oz. fat-free Greek yogurt

4   oz. fat-free cream cheese, room temperature

4   oz. carrot baby food

1   egg + 2 egg whites

¼   c. natural maple syrup

1   tsp. vanilla

INSTRUCTIONS

1.   Preheat oven to 375 degrees.

2.   Mix together all dry ingredients. Beat together all wet ingredients.
     Stir wet ingredients into dry ingredients.

3.   Spray 8x11 baking pan. Spread brownie mix in pan.

4.   Bake for 20 to 25 minutes or until a knife inserted into brownies comes out clean.

5.   Let cool. Cut into 12 bars.

"Try these and see if you can fool any brownie lover into choosing this healthier option! Why eat all the extra calories when you can make the sin-free version? I love to cut these into small bites and savor each one."

Nutritional Value
Nutritional information is based on 1 bar.

Calories: 85   Fat: 1g   Carbohydrates: 12g   Protein: 4g   Sugar: 3g

mini carrot cake muffins

Makes 48 mini muffins.

INGREDIENTS

- 2 c. whole-wheat flour
- ½ c. brown sugar
- ¼ c. olive oil
- ¼ c. applesauce
- ½ c. plain, fat-free Greek yogurt
- 2 tsp. cinnamon
- ¼ tsp. sea salt
- 2 tsp. baking powder
- 2 c. grated carrot
- 1 c. crushed pineapple
- 1 egg
- 3 egg whites
- 1 Tbsp. zest of orange
- 1 small container Cool Whip®
- 1 small container fat-free cream cheese
  (if desired for a creamier frosting/topping)

INSTRUCTIONS

1. Preheat oven to 350 degrees. Line mini-muffin tin with paper liners.

2. Beat eggs. Add sugar and oil. Add remaining ingredients. Mix well.

3. Pour into mini-muffin cups. Bake for 20 minutes.

4. Top each muffin with a dollop of Cool Whip and enjoy!

> *Try whipping ½ c. fat-free cream cheese with 1 cup Fat-Free Cool Whip for a more frosting-like topping. Just add a dollup, and enjoy!*

Nutritional Value
Nutritional information is based on 1 muffin.

Calories: 65   Fat: 2g   Carbohydrates: 10g   Protein: 2g   Sugar: 5g

With Whipped Topping

Calories: 83   Fat: 2g   Carbohydrates: 10g   Protein: 2g   Sugar: 6g

mini strawberry cheesecake bites

Makes about 15 servings.

INGREDIENTS

4   oz. fat-free cream cheese

4   oz. fat-free Greek yogurt

15   baked mini phyllo shells

15   whole strawberries, fresh or frozen

7   packets stevia or ¼ c. sugar

½   tsp. vanilla

1   Tbsp. balsamic vinegar

INSTRUCTIONS

1.   Bring cream cheese and yogurt to room temperature.
     Mix balsamic vinegar and two packets of sweetener
     (1 Tbsp. sugar). Pour over strawberries and mix well.

2.   Beat together cream cheese, yogurt, vanilla and
     remaining sweetener until creamy.

3.   Fill phyllo shells ¾ full with cheese mixture.
     Put 1 strawberry in shell and gently push down
     until inserted into cheese mixture.

4.   Chill for 1 hour, and enjoy!

hint:

These freeze well. Make lots ahead of time and freeze. When you go to a party, simply take desired amount out of freezer, thaw and people will beg for the recipe! Always keep a supply on hand in the freezer. When you get that urge for something sweet, grab 1 or 2 and you will satisfy that craving without eating a lot of calories or fat.

Nutritional Value
Nutritional information is based on 1 cheesecake bite.

Calories: 32   Fat: 1g   Carbohydrates: 3g   Protein: 2g   Sugar: 2g

maple pumpkin cheesecake

Makes about 9 servings.

INGREDIENTS

12	oz. fat-free cream cheese
½	c. natural maple syrup
½	c. fat-free Greek yogurt or fat-free sour cream
½	tsp. vanilla
2	eggs
2	egg whites
8	oz. canned pumpkin (not pie mix, just plain pumpkin)
¾-1	tsp. ground cinnamon
⅛-¼	tsp. ground nutmeg

INSTRUCTIONS

1. Preheat oven to 375 degrees.

2. Beat cream cheese and syrup until smooth. Blend in yogurt, vanilla and spices. Beat in eggs one at a time. Beat in egg whites. Blend in pumpkin until smooth.

3. Pour into an 8 x 8 baking dish and bake for about 25 to 30 minutes or until cheesecake is set.

4. Cool and refrigerate for at least 4 hours. Cut into 9 square pieces. You also can cut into 1-inch squares and serve as an appetizer or mini dessert.

Nutritional Value
Nutritional information is based on 1/9 of cheesecake.

Calories: 76   Fat: 1g   Carbohydrates: 6g   Protein: 9g   Sugar: 2g

cranberry treat

Makes 6 servings.

INGREDIENTS

- 12 oz. bag frozen cranberries
- ½ c. white wine
- 12 packets stevia or ½ c. sugar
- 1 package unflavored gelatin
- ⅔ c. lukewarm water
- 6 oz. fat-free cream cheese
  pecan pieces (optional)

INSTRUCTIONS

1. Put frozen cranberries in nonstick sauce pan. Add wine and simmer until cranberries burst and are creamy (stirring a few times while simmering).

2. Add gelatin to water and let sit for a few minutes.

3. Remove cranberry mixture from heat and stir in sweetener. Stir in gelatin water and cream cheese. Mix thoroughly.

4. Pour into six ½ c. ramekins. Sprinkle with a few pecan pieces, if desired.

5. Cover and put in refrigerator until cooled and firm. Serve cold.

Nutritional Value
Nutritional information is based on 1 ramekin.

Calories: 77　　Fat: 0g　　Carbohydrates: 63g　　Protein: 5g　　Sugar: 4g

miscellaneous

banana chocolate almond butter shake

Makes 1 serving.

INGREDIENTS

1	scoop of vanilla whey protein (recommended brand: Isagenix)
½-1	Tbsp. almond butter
½	small banana (prefer frozen)
2	tsp. cocoa powder
½-¾	c. ice cubes
¾	c. cold water

INSTRUCTIONS

1. Place ingredients in a blender and blend until smooth.

Nutritional Value
Nutritional information is based on 1 shake.

Calories: 210 ❁ Fat: 6g ❁ Sodium: 90mg ❁ Carbohydrates: 20g ❁ Fiber: 4g ❁ Sugar: 9g ❁ Protein: 23g

pumpkin pie shake

Makes 1 serving.

INGREDIENTS

1	scoop of vanilla whey protein (recommended brand: Isagenix)
1	Tbsp. canned coconut milk
2	Tbsp. canned pumpkin puree (prefer frozen)
½	small banana (prefer frozen)
¾	tsp. pumpkin pie spice
	dash of cinnamon
½-¾	c. ice cubes
¾	c. cold water

INSTRUCTIONS

1. Place ingredients in a blender and blend until smooth.

Nutritional Value
Nutritional information is based on 1 shake.

Calories: 205 ❁ Fat: 5g ❁ Sodium: 95mg ❁ Carbohydrates: 21g ❁ Fiber: 3g ❁ Sugar: 10g ❁ Protein: 19g

mocha delicious shake

Makes 1 serving.

INGREDIENTS

- 1 scoop of vanilla whey protein (recommended brand: Isagenix)
- ½ small banana (prefer frozen)
- ½ Tbsp. nut butter (optional)
- 2 tsp. cocoa powder
- ½ c. cold coffee
- ¼ c. water
- ½ c. ice cubes

INSTRUCTIONS

1. Place ingredients in a blender and blend until smooth.

Nutritional Value
Nutritional information is based on 1 shake.

Calories: 215 ❀ Fat: 7g ❀ Sodium: 95mg ❀ Carbohydrates: 19g ❀ Fiber: 3g ❀ Sugar: 9g ❀ Protein: 20g

creamy blueberry avocado shake

Makes 1 serving.

INGREDIENTS

- 1 scoop of vanilla whey protein (recommended brand: Isagenix)
- ¼ avocado
- ½ frozen banana
- ¼ c. blueberries (fresh or frozen)
- ¼ tsp. ground nutmeg
- 1 Tbsp. canned coconut milk
- ⅓ c. coconut water (can use water)
- ¾ c. cold water
- ½-¾ c. ice cubes

INSTRUCTIONS

1. Place ingredients in a blender and blend until smooth.

Nutritional Value
Nutritional information is based on 1 shake.

Calories: 285 ❀ Fat: 10g ❀ Sodium: 100mg ❀ Carbohydrates: 29g ❀ Fiber: 5g ❀ Sugar: 15g ❀ Protein: 20g

basil & cottage cheese pesto

Makes 12 servings.

Submitted by Sibyl Smith of Virginia

INGREDIENTS

- 2 cloves garlic
- ½ c. basil
- 1 c. 2% cottage cheese
- ¼ tsp. Kosher salt
- juice of ½ a lemon
- 1 Tbsp. olive oil
- ¼ c. freshly grated Parmesan cheese

INSTRUCTIONS

1. Combine all ingredients in food processor or blender.

Nutritional Value

Nutritional information is based on 2 Tbsp.

Calories: 38 • Fat: 2g • Sodium: 150mg • Carbohydrates: 1g • Fiber: 0g • Sugar: 0g • Protein: 3g

whole-wheat bread crumbs

INGREDIENTS

1   loaf low-calorie, 100% whole-wheat bread
(I use Healthy Life® bread — 35 calories per slice)

INSTRUCTIONS

1. Preheat oven to 350 degrees.

2. Cut crust off of bread. Put in food processor or blender, and blend to a fine crumb consistency.

3. Spread out on jelly roll pan, and spray with olive oil cooking spray.

4. Bake in oven, stirring occasionally, until bread crumbs are dry and lightly brown.

hint:

Freezes well in plastic storage bags. Excellent for all recipes calling for bread crumbs. You can add garlic salt and Italian seasoning to spice up the bread crumbs to your liking.

Nutritional Value
Nutritional information is based on 1 cup.

Calories: 110   Fat: 0g   Carbohydrates: 17g   Protein: 8g   Sugar: 3g

parmesan crisps

Makes 16 servings.

INGREDIENTS

1   c. grated Parmesan cheese
¼   tsp. garlic powder
⅛   tsp. chili powder

INSTRUCTIONS

1. Preheat oven to 350 degrees.

2. Mix spices with Parmesan cheese.

3. Drop 1 Tbsp. of cheese on baking sheet.

4. Bake for 3 to 5 minutes until edges of
    cheese are lightly brown. Let cool.

> *"Take any old dish or salad and make it impressive by adding this simple
> garnish. These are great as an appetizer, too!"*

Nutritional Value
Nutritional information is based on 1 crisp.

Calories: 21   ❋   Fat: 2g   ❋   Carbohydrates: 0g   ❋   Protein: 2g   ❋   Sugar: 0g

whole-wheat croutons

INGREDIENTS

3   slices whole-wheat, low-calorie bread

    cooking spray

¼   tsp. garlic salt

1   Tbsp. grated Parmesan cheese

INSTRUCTIONS

1. Preheat oven to 325 degrees.

2. Cut crust off of bread. Cut bread into ½-inch x ½-inch cubes.

3. Spread out on jelly roll pan and spray with cooking spray.

4. Sprinkle with garlic salt and parmesan.

5. Bake in oven, stirring occasionally, for 10 to 12 minutes until croutons are dry and lightly brown.

6. Store in air tight container and use on all your salads and soups for that extra crunch!

tip:

Let your taste buds be your guide! Experiment with other herbs and seasonings to change the flavor of the croutons — there are so many options!

Nutritional Value
Nutritional information is based on 1 cup.

Calories: 105   Fat: 0g   Carbohydrates: 17g   Protein: 6g   Sugar: 3g

index

Be sure to visit www.loriharder.com for more fast, fun and easy recipes!